FLORILEGIUM

FLORILEGIUM

*poems
with a glossary*

———————————

by

MOLLY VOGEL

SHEARSMAN BOOKS

First published in the United Kingdom in 2020 by
Shearsman Books Ltd
PO Box 4239
Swindon
SN3 9FN

Shearsman Books Ltd Registered Office
30–31 St. James Place, Mangotsfield, Bristol BS16 9JB
(this address not for correspondence)

www.shearsman.com

ISBN 978-1-84861-702-5

Copyright © Molly Vogel, 2020.

The right of Molly Vogel to be identified as the author
of this work has been asserted by her in accordance with the
Copyrights, Designs and Patents Act of 1988.
All rights reserved.

Cover design by Vanessa Romrell.

To Thomas

CONTENTS

I

The Gloaming	13
The Lightening	14
On Heidegger's *Being and Time*	16
Elegy for Emma	17
Light Iris, 1924	19
Snow Bunting	21
Una Ursula	22
Penny Wedding	23
Ode to Neruda	24
Flora and Fauna	27
My Mother the Dishwasher	29

II *Metamorphosis*

Interruption and Completion of a Thought	33
The Artist Moved to Despair	
at the Grandeur of Antique Fragments	34
Birdbook	35
Bashō's Prefaces to the Novels of Henry James	36
Verse-Riddles	38
Interludes	39
Glasgow Haiku	40
Some Definitions	41
Listening to Scriabin for the First Time	43
The Dog	44
Colloquy with a Closed Window	45
Sunday	49
Danaë	50

III

Antonyms	53
Lot's Wife	55
No Hay Olvido	56
The Gallery	58
Lorem Ipsum	59
La Collectionneuse	60
Oceanic	62
Dies Natalis	63
Lessons on How to Understand a Famous Painting	64
Isle of Skye	65
Schliesse mir die Augen beide	66
Orchid	69
The Child Dreaming in a Poet's House	70
Stabat Mater	71
Glesga Prayer	73
The Loves of Plants	75
GLOSSARY	77
ACKNOWLEDGEMENTS	122

Every bird that sings, and every bud that blooms, does but remind me more of that garden unseen, awaiting the hand that tills it.

—Emily Dickinson

J'ai seulement fait ici un amas de fleurs étrangères, n'y ayant fourni du mien que le filet à les lier.

I have gathered a posy of other men's flowers, and nothing but the thread that binds them is mine own.

—Michel de Montaigne

I

THE GLOAMING

    Stepping lightly, the gloaming catches
in the throat; thick tufts of wheat catch
    lightly. The song thrush calls

    the day is ending. The scythe rests.
Memory gleans east of the canal
    as father and son kneel in a field.

    The alfalfa sends up their prayers
as seeds in wind, in hushed succession.
    Brownie, the pony, watches stilly.

    In a dream, he would see you in France, wounded,
in a field of mustard. The dream came thrice
    as a shutter on the heart. He did not know

    it was your footing; a plea for the lead
to miss any poor soul. An oath between man
    and his God levels the field.

    He knows you by your name. He sees
the work, and deems it fine. The strands
    of wheat on the whetstone

    are as the down of a babe—
the same hands work both with equal
    discernment. You now dream of the redcurrant bush

    —how you split it like the rood in pieces
across the yard, little garnets come spring,
    and mother in her apron pleased

    —that we are more than the sum
of our parts. Body grafted to spirit
    and you—to Margaret.

THE LIGHTENING

The place where the mind goes—
        in grief, I am led invisibly
to summers in Meadow Vista,

minnows clustered on the lake—
        Margaret takes my hand
to the blackberry bush.

In childish instancy, I do not see
        the thorns, only
deep garnets. We climb a ladder

to the highest bramble. We sneak
        several in our mouths. And later—
jam with the same hand.

What urgency is God's work
        (who will plant the daffodils
next spring?)

—the burgundy petals of each
        dahlia catch the light, the sum
of these days

is reticent. Flower heads nod
        soundless in the wind
the birds song soundless—

Margaret, with whom I share
        a name, I have
engraved you on the palms

of my hands—with blackberry juice
    —with needle and thread
—with child.

Now, what is left but quiet presence
    in time,
the leaf turns, a deer

crosses the blue-oak forest, like light
    you can step in
and out of.

ON HEIDEGGER'S *BEING AND TIME*

    I
When I was fourteen, I wanted to play the violin. I did not
have the discipline of my twin, her feet
dragging before her eyes down each stair early
before seminary each morning. My Mom would accompany her
on the piano, a remnant from girlhood that came before
books and boys. Vanessa would play while she thought,
and Mom thought I slept upstairs.
I was listening: a book by my bedside and my black lab asleep
with me in my twin bed.

Now, I would hear Mother say. It is time, *now* is the time. Everyone
is waiting for you. Your siblings are waiting for you
in the car. God is waiting for you, too.

    II
The metronome tsks time. It is the telling of the *now*,
now, now, now. It is the quiet from the before,
the clamor of what is to come: four equally stressed
sixteenths. The details deliberate, the need for discipline
in the disparate. The phrasing of it all, time being robbed
from one note to another. There is refuge in order.
The absoluteness of a thing holding time, holding time
in time. It is pointing to *now*, no, *now*, though the tick-tick sound
has come and gone before it has come.

    III
Listen: one can only wait
for nothing and nothing waits
for no one. I know nothing
and know no end.

ELEGY FOR EMMA

I

Today I pass the time plucking
oranges from your tree,
dropping them one by one
into a trash bin
with a hole
in the bottom.

I walk through
your house breathing
the bitter scent of it
and leave its letters
falling into a bowl on your table.

It feels like a dream:
the skin of the fruit
in my hand,
the slivers of half-moons
taking shape
in my mouth
and still (so late
in the season)
there is fruit
on the trees.

II

I stand in the silence
of your kitchen,
the cupboards empty,
their contents growing tired
in a brown box:
olive green plates
from your wedding,

a rusted silver spoon,
derby cups from 1951,
a wine glass,
and a clock
without the time.

You didn't drink
I say to no one.
And I didn't know you liked horses.

A painting of some Bolshevik village
rests clumsily off its hook
next to a photo of a nameless couple.
I ask mom who that woman is.
She says your grandmother.
It is her wedding day
and even in the black and white,
in the shadows of her lace collar,
the folds of her dress, in the creases
of her darkly lined eyes and lips,
her face drifts
to the surface
a budding lily.

LIGHT IRIS, 1924
Georgia O'Keeffe, water colour

    I
Your slender limbs grow,
only when planted. Your slender limbs,
growing.

I want to grow
with you, to entwine
with your roots

in dark unfurling
over
and over me.

    II
When I want
to be myself,
I hide; put my hands

in pockets
or learn to love
my body softly, sometimes

touching,
imposing on everything
and nothing.

    III
I want to feel skin.
I want to feel the skin
of skin. I branch my fingers,

spread them thin, nesting
in the small of your back.
I want to nest. In you,

I am planted; your petal,
your pollen, I would like
to be.

      IV
I feel the weight of hands
carrying a plant
that never blooms.

SNOW BUNTING

When I plucked you from your aerie
that was *leave in the wind*.
Someone must have entered
an empty room.

The walls spit feathers.
We did not reach the long
and low sleep of martyrs.

Since despair is my forsaker,
and you my keeper, I confess
(*mea maxima culpa*). For your part

in this sorry slip of hearts,
you should sit on Càrn Dearg alone.
For mine, I will keep company with excess

out on the bird-shore,
our rapine bodies sore
in their longings.

The grey day's aria hums through our wrinkled bones.

UNA URSULA
for Robinson Jeffers

You have been so quiet for so long;
    forty-some odd years
Sweep by, weed-barren and hushed, nestled in
The neck of a hollow. Your father, dark-eyed,
Holy-laden, ebbed and flowed by dawning,
As if he had meant not to be seen. You prefer
Evening, swollen and thickening by full-tide,
    a terrible moon beautiful and down-cast,
Revelling in itself and its callous
Blue. Despite herself, Ursula glows brightest, your little-bear,
    fiery and merciless in the throat of the sky.
It is so easy to remember a time when things were not so
Beautiful. You sipped red wine
And I drank Irish whiskey, as if the perils of
Death were not enough. Instead, you learned to make
    stone love stone
And adorned the wild
Hawk with sympathy; find mercy in your god-like
Thirst for the delicate and the desolate.
When you said life's end is death, I am not certain
    you meant it. For although the haven of sea-
Fog, its cold-snare ambushing Tor House, returns
By way of the torrent river, you do not know whom to give
The poem to now that it is written.

PENNY WEDDING

Stepping stone; an archipelago of moss
covered turtle shells. What is lost

over the border, over a skein
of seaweed. The sea negotiates

with qualms, an ineptitude for depth,
flotsam measured itself starboard;

a brother in Assisi flecks coins
among the flourishing machair.

Golden poppies exchange glances;
a nod or two in light

of the above. Taken into account
centaury, gentian, eyebright—

sentinels of Calafia and, scattered,
exchequers of manna.

ODE TO NERUDA

You, Pablo,
wrote with sea-
green ink,
only, you said,
because it was
the colour of
Esperanza.

I'd like to think
your fingers
were vines,
or rivers that poured
over leaves
and leaves
of poetry.
Five syllables, each
to a finger:
one the sea
over broken glass
contemplating
the tide.
Another, maybe,
a bell. Its shape
resonates
Matilde.

Did you hide
your hands
in your pockets?
Did they fall
heavy
at your side,
exhausted by the old
rickety sway
of your body,

or did they grow
tired of the paper,
words thick
as molasses?

Are you embarrassed
by the fragility
of your own
hands?
For each knuckle,
each tender
tendon.
Your ten muses.

You feel at home
touching wool.
You savour
the way
the tips of your fingers sound coarse
and calloused,
just spelling it.

Or maybe
they wrote best
when nested
in the curve
of a woman's
hip.
At last,
the tips
dance
like caterpillars.
One would have
guessed
you played
the piano.

You, Pablo,
your words
are always
philosophizing
in my mind,
like apple slices
conversing,
trying to remember
a time
being whole.

Your words
are book
and bookend.
For when my mouth
is filled with
your name,
in between my skull
and the sea
that fills me,
I want to say
manzana,
or even risk
Neruda.
Doesn't that sound
so sweet.

FLORA AND FAUNA

    I
on highway seventeen to the northeast
side of aptos toward soquel
there meets two creeks
sempervirens falls
into big-basin near
the chaparral pea

    II
i am thinking your body could be
california: it is the same sharp-shinned
hawk your mouth red huckleberries
your hair feathers
on the dark-eyed junco
quietly in the redwood tree

    III
wild (at our first) beasts words
—our coming makes stones sing like birds—
but o the starhushed silence which ours thirsts
you and i in my thinnest dress
the root-knot path
in green chinquapin thirds

    IV
let us lurch and press in the woods
and i will make a dress of your words—
redwood violet, little trillium, my mountain iris
speak to me the costanoan language
make me your *mukurma* woman
sii water taste me like *oo'-rahk* salmon

V
a would-home of knob-cone
pines my love (cheeks flush
like bush poppies)

MY MOTHER THE DISHWASHER

My mother the dishwasher had hands
like gnarled roots, like the old oak

sighing out back. Nearly everything that grew
was a product of her hands.

And so her spade fell into earth. Azaleas
and poppies flushed at the sight of her.

She grew nothing for herself. Her limbs
would only limply lie in soapy water.

Watching mother's hands rise and fall
with each soiled pot and pan, I thought

I would see tulip bulbs burst. I thought
that if I knew the secrets of her sowing,

of the sadness in her fingertips, of her
sinews, the dishes would become

invisible. And maybe if I held them—if I slipped
my hand into mother's the way my father

slipped his into hers thirty-some years ago,
I would become invisible, too.

II
Metamorphosis

INTERRUPTION AND COMPLETION OF A THOUGHT

In class, the shared-desk, you are next
to me. I am trying to think
of the last line to a haiku:
black hair
kuro kami no
tangled in a thousand strands
chisuji no kami no
tangled my hair and
midaregami
tangled my tangled memories
omoi midare katsu

My love
we wade into holiness
wait in loneliness
the weight-stone of blessed duress.

Stillness: a single finger slips down the neck
of my boot, and still—
our long nights of love-making
omoi midaruru.

THE ARTIST MOVED TO DESPAIR AT
THE GRANDEUR OF ANTIQUE FRAGMENTS
Henry Fuseli, 1778–79

Solitary foot,   we cannot know your mythic body,
fleece-skin, bone chalk, the crescent nail…

    I worship the illusion of you.
I entered your house and have washed your limbs
with tears, wiped them with my hair
unmarred: the monolith burns from the inside out.
    Dwell in the idea of man's image
and the missing mouth will speak unfettered,

  pour forth my soul
and the fire quickens within me.   Trivial

rag-weed: towards eternity, a finger.

BIRDBOOK

I
a crow
in the rhododendron

II
it is the bird's hour
a cry
the size of a wren
is left to sleep
in the margins
of our bed

III
bitter bird
what do we do
with the body

for its sake
i draw a line between it
and the heavens

IV
we watch the sky gone
under the flight
of a flightless bird

V
the song of a swallow
loosens my ribboned tongue
in this moment
your silence is understood best

BASHŌ'S PREFACES
TO THE NOVELS OF HENRY JAMES

'The Portrait of a Lady'

Curve of the Riva,
the little hunchbacked bridges
rise and drop again

one wave upon wave—
tap and click of pedestrians.
Venetian footfall

calls across water:
recall the particular
sedum of summer.

'Daisy Miller'

See: what artistry
grants the fair flower of sense
to the pure poet?

Let us arrange these
blossoms in a bowl—
mark of felicity.

'The Wings of the Dove'

Through a glass darkly,
woman is a long shadow
this winter evening.

The mystic figure?
Here at your grave flowers
an empty road.

VERSE-RIDDLES

        I

My neck, iron-clad; head cast sharp by the forge
of chisels. I change shape to stay the same. Place me
agape inside an open mouth and I strain against pointed
teeth. Cast your bit wisely: it is I who stand between
my Lord and his kingdom. Break me and never know
my promise; knock and it shall not be opened unto you.

        II

Silent is my dress when I bow to earth; pluck me
for pleasure and watch me blush; witness the birth of neither
nymph nor satyr. I am barren with seeds; watch me dismantle
my own throat. Who savors me pressed in wind? My vellum
pinion spews life. Shorn, my woolly husk unfurls
like a mollusk. I stand singular with many, mimic of mimicry.

INTERLUDES

      I
early morning,
no clothes, a boy
sees me through
the window and
smiles

      II
a few empty chairs:
the statues have moved into
museum corners.

      III
blue pomegranate
halved in the night you are still
spilling stars

GLASGOW HAIKU

I
after Bashō

auld dub—
a puddock plops
tae wade the watter

II
the ither nicht
anely hoffway hame
doon it came all
plump like.
jus pissn.
an nae coat.
jist shows ye disnae,
jist goes to show ye.

SOME DEFINITIONS
w. ref. to Geoffrey Hill

Beauty. "He who loves the beautiful is called a lover because he partakes of it." See *Phaedrus* 249 E as the midwife of the soul. The ladder is always there. The words are maps. We are dealing with a phantom. I could speak about the thing more autobiographically; it's the emphasis where one is most likely to be questioned, n'est-ce pas?

Bird. The derivation of the word *augur* is uncertain; ancient authors believed that it contained the words *avi* and *gero*, Latin for "directing the birds"—but historical-linguistic evidence points instead to the root *aug-*, "to increase, to prosper". Only a few birds could give auguries among the Romans (Cic. *de Div.* II. 34). You can be air since I am bird.

California. Calafia: *Las sergas de Esplandián*, 1500. "Know ye that at the right hand of the Indies there is an island called California, very close to that part of the Terrestrial Paradise, which was inhabited by black women without a single man among them, and they lived in the manner of Amazons." They were robust of body with strong passionate hearts and great virtue.

Dactyl. For the association of the metrical foot, late 14c., from Gk *dactylos*, literally "finger" (also "toe"); origin unknown; a long syllable followed by two shorts analogous with the three joints of a finger.

Oak. A magical tree. I remember a dream: a twelve-year-old boy has fallen asleep under a tree. In time, the tree grows old. Think of the body's loneliness. You sleep to stay alive. The tree and the boy are inseparable. How long did you lie amongst the acorns? In a poem, you bring them all together.

Self. "One is right to distrust the opinion that associates self with self-expression, as if the self-expression were ectoplasm emanating in a tenuous stream from the allegedly authentic self. One's idea of the authentic self may be quite different from the authentic self as it really is. The dividing line between innocent stupidity and fakery is very unclear; that innocent stupidity and deliberate fakery can coexist in the one writer."

Truth. See Giovanni di Paulo's *St Thomas Aquinas Confounding Averroës.* There is one truth, but at least two ways to reach it. The world is eternal, the soul divided. See "monopsychism". If I remember rightly, the synopsis said that St Thomas is refuting Averroës, and that Averroës is writhing in pain and distress on the floor. To me he looked peacefully asleep.

LISTENING TO SCRIABIN
FOR THE FIRST TIME

No eye has seen, nor ear heard; neither have entered
into the heart. The things that are prepared for us
that love. I am thinking
about Eve in the garden, how in her solitude
she was tempted. How everything comes back
to Eve. Her lonely image reflected in a pool.

(What there thou seest fair creature is thy self.)

I remember learning how Milton found
he could no longer see, how he recited the poem
to his three daughters for ten years (*without whom am
to no end*) from the confines of his memory. I think
of you now, alone, in your room, listening.

THE DOG
Francisco Goya, 1819–1823

The mount fades into black.
Fall or rise
Denies the question, the frame ends without.

A shadow leaves a line of itself.
Eclipsed
Dog the colour of dirt,

Grain, ochre—
Listen for the call
Between the calls echo,

Prayer is left out.
Stay, the far
Light is a broken halo.

COLLOQUY WITH A CLOSED WINDOW

1 AUBADE

I   In my lap   a closed *Harmonium*. Its yellowed jacket
        recalls butter-milk poppies. Covered in a funeral
procession of words, it could be a publisher's last memo. My bedfellow
for three days   I carry it with me in the space of Santa Cruz: hyperion
tree, to Mass (no accident!); I've been taking it to the zoo (to get acquainted),
and—finally—I wake with the first sun   in my eyes, it
   lying open   on my chest.

Thanks to an age-old jealousy, an inability to love in twos, I lightly doggy-ear
        a page   or two: 'I am content when wakened birds, before
they fly, test the reality
of misty fields, by their sweet questionings.'   A nod
            and a page or two fleeting encounters.

II   As much a book of silences as chirpings.

III   The first I could do when I had swallowed it whole was take a long
        nap. I was caught in amber   as captured light.
Light: the whole sky onto my head, a blue sets blue round, down onto the
        naked backs of tops.

I listen for an answer: look at the lilacs. From a distance his page looks
   blank: empty space. (No need to worry.) He is all   wide open, a
door   off its hinges.

Step into the lightening

and a bird becomes the only exhalation: 'when the blackbird flew out of

sight, it marked the edge' (the edge)

                'of one   of many circles.'

      A radiant weight.

IV   Light. On one

          side of a line. In true fashion: 'an up and down
between two elements
a fluctuating between sun and moon.'

          Chiaroscuro

all bottled up in a jar: the jar of every day, the jarring everyday

          I fling open   the book: refracting light.

  An alchemist: 'the spring is like a belle undressing.'

Further, farther: 'the gold tree is blue, the singer has pulled his cloak over his head. The moon

  is in the folds of the cloak.'

V   blue: imagination
        tawny: reality
        green: body
        aureolin: sun
        taupe: mirth

furniture for the page.

VI   A simple matter of trust: what is written is life. You can't avoid it.

2 METAMORPHOSIS

The light dove, cleaving the air in her free flight, and feeling its resistance, might imagine that its flight would be still easier in empty space.
　　　　　　　—Immanuel Kant

I　　I listen to the bray of my heart:
　　　iamb,　　iamb,　　iamb.

3 NOCTURNE

et lux in tenebris lucet, et tenebræ eam non comprehenderunt

I From the balcony, a relic suspended
    on air. There are other signs
    that light beseeched us: incense arrives
    in the most easterly corner.
    An uncurled flame strikes the veil
    turning granite into gold. It will become one
    of many. So the sun rose from shoulders
    of a congregation: the desert, the small
    yellowing village, the light dove.
    You sit somewhere else
    instructing me in the dark:

> *Saint Columba*
> *Saint Ninian*
> *Saint Margaret of Scotland*

> *Saint Joseph*
> *Saint David*
> *Saint Catherine of Siena*

II When many gods in the shape
    of a small shrine
    approached me in the mouth
    of a room, I was frightened; then I saw servitude
    in praise. I lit a flame eclipsed
    speaking a strange language.
    Who might be watching?
    Then it didn't matter.

SUNDAY
after Marina Tsvetaeva

Broken with worry, God
paused for me.
And look, there were many
prayers with bodies

In a word I had
given them,
Some with large wings and
others without any.

I weep because
why so much.
Even more than God
himself I love his.

DANAË
Gustav Klimt, 1907

It's been
thousands
upon thousands
of years of gold.
I was a god,
and this is what I did,
striking
without hands,
or hammer,
piercing
without needle,
without tools other
than gold,
gold,
the colour gold.

III

ANTONYMS

I

As a girl, I dreamed
of cotton. The inside
of the boll shaped like a tiny
skull would grow moist,
malleable fibres, which would push
out from the skin
of the newly formed seeds
like strings of pearls. As the boll
ripened, it would turn a barren
brown. The fibres would continue
to expand under the sun's warmth
until finally, they would split
the boll apart and the thick cotton
would burst forth between the shell
like grey matter from the head. I would awake
startled by this image in the dead
of night, a slight pressure
behind my temples, in between my ears,
deep inside my belly. I imagine
the whites of my eyes as cotton ground to a pulp,
chalky as crushed bone, the kind you can taste,
the bitterness lingers on the tip of your tongue
like phosphate, like a
sharp tooth.

II

My Father was a coal
miner, his heart as black as the earth
he robbed. I would later remember
Father falling one hundred and fifty feet
to his death down the throat
of a shaft, to the underbelly of a colliery,
his body mangled by the rocks
he had grown fond of. His limp body would be
obscured by thick dust and loose rubble, wedged
in between two large rocks that would prevent
the miners from retrieving his body
for five days. It is said Father had struck a vein,
a vein so deep, so old that when he fell
into the dark pit, and cracked his
skull, the blood ran black.

LOT'S WIFE
after Szymborska

Memory has what it sought.
It is customary to hear her breathe
the breath of Jehovah.

He has already forgotten
his neck does not feel
many-eyed fear.

For want of eternity ten thousand
grains have been composed.
She has the look of one just born.

Her eyes might be open.
The salt-crown has outlasted the head.
She is not a statue, but a mound.

If anyone had seen her,
they might have thought her holy.
One breath—she is gone.

NO HAY OLVIDO

If you should ask me where I have been
   all this time
I would say 'At sea'. I am too alone in this world
  yet not   alone
     enough   to make every hour holy. I am
much too much in this world,
 yet not much
    enough
to be to you thing or object. I have been meaning
  to mean   nothing for awhile, except, for example,

'This is
the same night

whitening the same trees.' This is the long silence
  from which everything begins and from which everything
ends.

                          The bird   takes flight,
   the oak   grows old.

Should you ask me where I come from
   I can only speak using broken things, say, perhaps,

'The clock wakes us
     past twelve-thirty;
discarded clothes
      scatter
the floor
  shed from our
bodies like
book sleeves;
    we make our bed.'
    We make do with
broken things.

   Love: all that we are lives in the body
of a word   *tantas cosas que*
quiero olvidar. (I know not what to question,
there are so many dead answers.)

I want to be a blessing of being.
I want to unwant some memory

 like a word new I learned,
like the everyday sleep,
 like the California fern,
like my tongue a tall weed.

THE GALLERY

It is withholding for the last time. For the last time, your hands wander
my body as we sit with our selves, birch bench, a thread of your hair

in my mouth. This time your body makes me think of breath
the way I learned to swim. Look how you unfold, old-saint, late-love,

God's last hymn. I and my Glasgow boys: Christ of Saint John,
1901 cherrywood organ, Mackintosh, and you are a song in my ear,

you say, with grace, with-holding, with unknown knowing. Dearest one,
tecum vivere amem, tecum obeam libens. It is the language I think in

as we press hard limbs. All the color tastes like blood in my mouth (skin
on skin). This time your breath makes me think of body the way

I first drank red wine. Look how you open (and close), you say, divine-
dolmen, rejoiced in sin, little kiss-sighs. Your hands are prayers

for my thighs. All the while, we discuss Brueghel the Elder with salty tongues,
the unhinged crucifix, life's psalm. A toddler watches with his father.

LOREM IPSUM

So this is what Thursday looks like
with you, the stillness of the marble
statues, koi in a pond, water lily

perched, like artichoke
on a plate. Brief rain makes a crown
of your hair, while a dog-

wood makes it snow in June.
Somewhere, a window is open
to laundry on a line and full-hipped tulips

skirt their way across a field. The wind, too, nods
a branch into approval, skimming an edge
off the river with a bony finger

where it points to the end of a fishing line
negotiating with fish; I wait for water
to bloom sideways, a taut chord gesturing

to the boy on the bridge and plump clouds
become pillars, some invisible anchor
to separate sky from river—white petals,

a heron's wing span becomes a place-
holder for our eyes, its outline minueting
with the movement of every thing.

LA COLLECTIONNEUSE

I have been becoming more feline.
I consider the spots of sun streaming
through my flat more thoughtfully,
which patch to approach most leisurely,
which bit of light reflects off my book just so.
I even stripped down to the nude today.
I fell asleep for hours, pretending
I was floating on my back in open waters,
the window at eye-level and, hence,
where sea-level would be.
The sun stone-hot on my womanhood, I thought:
is this how the world began?
A big, blazing sore between the legs.
Splayed open in this way it was not a stretch
to imagine giving birth—
why did God create a part of us we cannot see?
Imagine it, the doctor, between my legs,
poking around and you
you on the other side of the partition
wanting my same no-view.
It's the not-knowing I don't like.
And so man created mirror in his image.
The cat, too, licks her wounds
in the shadow of a room.
Even she has had enough of the sun
for one day. It overwhelms you
to make the point of laziness
and, try as you might, you can't think
but on the very fact of it.
It is every where.
And thank God for that.
As a result, California is not far from the mind
and the time you laid yourself right out
on a zebra-print blanket in a mustard field.

Driving home weeks later
coming down a hill to be exact
you could have sworn you could
make out a patch, a square
outline on a distant mound;
who could see you
from this vantage point
for the brilliance of the sun?
The thought of your own white nakedness was blinding.
Had suburbia ever seen anything so open and vast?
The cat jumps at a flash of reflection;
shadows on a wall.
Once I watched this French film
about a guy who tries to do nothing.
It was recommended by another guy who never loved me.
It was all about the futility of finding absence.
See, he's in the south of France,
doing things that only people
in the south of France do:
reading, smoking, drinking wine, having women.
It's like an unfunny Seinfeld because somehow
nihilism is beautiful.
To try and do nothing is so close to surrendering to God.
One time, he walked in on me naked,
in bed, at five in the afternoon.
For shame of it, I pretended to be asleep.
I think he was startled, too.
And for fear of presence, he covered me up,
slipped a duvet right over me
and shut the door
to place distance between me and him
or him and me, I don't know which.

OCEANIC

Where we sat alone on a bench:
grey shadow cairn-shaped.

Far overhead, ribbons
of lochweed:

the soundless engine,
soundless engine of breath

and the wind
shouldering heads

of white flowers—our eyes
rolling on water.

A lamp
phosphorus,

our bodies full
of long distances, winter

keeps coming months early.
Each word sticks in the undertow.

The sad boats drift.
The children leave home.

Each night our sea-wreck, each day
waking into our skin.

DIES NATALIS

On this night, I look for some unknowing presence
of you in the sky: nothing. Not a star in sight.
Were you born by light or by the long silence
of darkness? I learn a new word today.
It ends before it begins, a seed planted too early
in the season. *Hyacinth shoots feather the ground
around my flat.* (I imagined that just as I imagine you
a pin-prick of light away. If I shut my eyes hard enough
you might be, too.) A field of sea asters; star-headed flowers
arranged in my field of vision. I rearrange the constellations
to mean something hidden, in true Nostradamus fashion.
(You share his birthday.) How careful God must be
with each point of sight. I trace miles with the edge
of two fingers and resist smouldering the small flame.
A sliver of light and your saint comes to mind.
I make meaning where there might be none.

LESSONS ON HOW TO UNDERSTAND A FAMOUS PAINTING
Self-Portrait, Albrecht Dürer

I. In this canvas, people have seen their husband, an accurate depiction of the Flemish people, a portrait of Martin Luther disguised as Albrecht Dürer, a coat I am intentionally wearing so I can comment aloud to others viewing the painting that I am wearing a similar coat to the one in the painting, or a vermillion ore that is found only in the nether regions of Madagascar which, when exposed to mercury, disintegrates into a million pieces, giving the artist the exact shade of green desired.

II. In only very rare circumstances has the painter been able to refer so deliberately to himself. Missing from the canvas is the mirror into which the artist gazes: half of it displays the artist adjusting his moustache, the other his non-existent trousers. His reflection does not surprise him; he has seen it many times and, in fact, likes it; but he is badly painted and reminds one of stale coffee, or a bad photograph of oneself that cannot be forgotten.

III. The methodical chestnut strokes filling the background have been frequently compared to chocolate, or the chattering leaves of fall. The truffle, a German delicacy, if eaten, would have killed him. How often Albrecht Dürer painted his own curls and felt the curve of the brush between his fingers, bending and aching quietly like a piano bench, or a creased page in a book. But it was already too late and the hair was finished. Albrecht knew it and sensed it was a terrible mistake.

IV. Step away from the canvas and this man is staring right at you. Take ten steps back and he appears familiar, as if you saw him once, but aren't sure where. Look closely. It appears he has written, 'It is fitting that a liar should be a man of good memory.' It might be the Devil who is saying these words and maybe you believe them because they are being spoken by a man who looks like Jesus.

ISLE OF SKYE

I wanted to know where love comes from
without you in the world, I am drowning
through the port at Mallaig, across thirty acres
of heathered heath, the old northeast glebe
keep my pockets full of flowers.
And then I remember: it is you
I miss in the fetterless body
of every living name: bluebell,
bog myrtle, yellow rattle,
thistle. You are every shade
of grey, root, and twinflower.
When love is not enough,
what is left but primrose, bearberry,
the weightless crux of water-lily?
The yew yawns a psalm,
the rood-bloom bows.
Tell me our story with/out
referent, with half-moon reverence.
I want to tell you what I couldn't say
most nights, take my hand along the edge
of it all is no line, only fond
foolishness, how I love the seriousness
of your fingers and the way you word
my half-name like amen. I stand
between white-beam and beech
like men. Where is my compass rose
amongst the rose garden?
Give all my longing to the River Brittle
down in the valley. There is no wait
in a flower, the too late bower.

SCHLIESSE MIR DIE AUGEN BEIDE
after Wittgenstein

1. If you do know *I love you*, I grant you all the rest.[1]
   When one says that such and such a proposition cannot be proved, of course that does not mean that it cannot be derived from other propositions; any proposition can be derived from other ones. But they may be no more certain than it is itself. (On this, a curious remark by A. Schopenhauer.)[2]

2. From its *seeming* to me—or to anyone—to be so, it does not necessarily follow that it is so. What we can ask is whether it would make sense to doubt it.

3. If someone says, e.g., 'I don't know if you love me', he might be told, 'look closer'—the possibility of satisfying oneself is part of the language-game.[3] This awareness is essential.

4. 'I know that I love you.' In order to see how unclear this proposition is, consider its negation. At most it might be taken to mean, 'Here, now, we forget each other and ourselves', or 'Not there but here (he whispers) only here'.[4] (Love, after all, the 'measurer past all measure'.) Can I doubt it? Grounds for doubt are sufficient. Everything speaks in its favour, nothing against it. Nevertheless it is imaginable 'this love will see me dead'.

5. Whether a proposition can turn out false depends on what I make count as determinants for that proposition.

---

[1] Read Plato's *Symposium*, 385–380 BC; see Weegee's *Lovers*, 1943; Antonio Canova's *Psyche Revived by Cupid's Kiss*, 1787; Henri de Toulouse-Lautrec's *Le lit*, 1893. Consider Henri Cartier-Bresson's *Swimming* (date unknown) at your leisure.

[2] *World as Will and Representation*, trans. by E. F. J. Payne, "2 vols (New York, NY: Dover, 1969), I, pp. 272–74."

[3] Read Ludwig Wittgenstein's *On Certainty*, 1969; hear Tom Waits' *Fawn, All the World is Green, Take It With Me*, 1999–2002; see Ingmar Bergman's *Sawdust and Tinsel*, 1953; Tod Browning's *The Unknown*, 1927, Federico Fellini's *La Strada*, 1954.

[4] Touch me.

6. Now, my love, can one enumerate what one knows? Perhaps not that quickly. The expression 'I know' is misused. And through misuse a strange mental state seems to be revealed.

7. My life shows that I know or am certain of what love is, love as is, the thing in itself, and so on—I tell someone e.g. 'I love you', etc., etc.

8. The difference between the concept of 'knowing' and the concept of 'being certain' is not of great importance except where 'I know' is meant to mean 'I cannot be wrong'. In a court of law, for example, 'I am certain' could replace 'I know' in every piece of testimony. We might even imagine it forbidden to say 'I know' there. (Consider a scene in *Pandora's Box*, 1929, where Lulu 'knew', instead of 'knows', the facts being different from what she knew at the time of trial.)

9. Now, do I, in the course of my life, make sure I know that here is love—what love is, that is? Yes.

10. I know a sick man is lying here? Nonsense! I am sitting at his bedside, I am looking attentively at his face. Neither the question nor the assertion makes any sense. No more than the assertion 'I am here', which I might yet use at any moment, if a suitable occasion were to present itself.

11. We just do not see how very specialized the use of 'I know' is.

12. For 'I know' seems to describe a state of guarantees of what is known, a state of facts. One always forgets the expression 'I thought I knew'.

13. 'I know' often means: I have the proper grounds for my statement. So if the other person is acquainted with the language-game, he would admit that I know. The other must be able to imagine *how* one may know something of that kind.[5]

---

[5] I like my body when it is with your body. I like its hows.

14. It would surely be remarkable if we had to believe the reliable person who says, 'I can't be wrong'.

15. I know I love you, and how.[6]

---

[6] I do not want to be wrong. Am I, therefore, unwilling to admit that my previous loves were/are untrue? I do not think that is necessarily the correct conclusion, but it must be considered and expanded upon later. Note: the most powerful word, God's creative word, is: be. But the most powerful word any human being has ever said is, if said by a lover: I abide. i.e., 'I abide'. Read S. Kierkegaard's *Works of Love*.

ORCHID

Everything I touch dies,
like your flowers,
the orchids.
They see me and
wilt, wilt, wilt
under the pressure
of my sorry hands. Their
stems could not stand.
Jaundiced, they tilt
stealing oxygen; the petals
charcoaled and bone dry
know my lies.
That is why they die.
When the white walls
seep carbon monoxide
and I fill cotton
in my mouth-hole
and I'm sick of all the words
I've stole, they
all, all, all
sweat out my pores.
One by one by one,
everything I touch dies.
My limbs are held together
by hook and eye,
and I am about to come undone.
That is why I dared not touch you
—but I did.
And you died too.
O, what am I to do,
what am I to do.

THE CHILD DREAMING IN A POET'S HOUSE
after Seferis

The flowering dark and the ravine which holds the moon waning
the papery lids close to the north wind like confetti and the wind
poppy vellum is skin between pages of a book; the stars are the sails of some
lost person. On the bedside sits the rind of the satsuma.

I have bridled my whole heart, a golden bit among apple orchards
on holy grass sweet the tall hierochloe is a bride, white throats pushing
up from wet stones in mud; dawn has two faces.
I have bridled my whole heart; on your left thigh a mark,
a basin creek at your knee, I have seen the long way your body
comes in from the rain, a great stone in bed, perhaps you exist
best sitting on a picket fence, a long line.

The face I see does not ask questions nor does the boy
watching from a distance. I climb the fence; I hold all of summer
in my hands. Beneath me the great body is flanked by bare feet,
no skein of rope. Into the distance I am gone with no line. The wheat
field folds over in my memory. Only fire on the peaks; they ask nothing
neither time a window frame nor sound. I have bridled my whole heart
on the silence of entire air. I don't have to speak.

I close my eyes to find the secret meeting place
under the breathing of the coast live oak
the tall grass against itself sounds like human voices
like the memory of your voice saying is there anything as still
as sleeping horses, there where the star lilies end, however hard
you try to recall your childhood years, however much you've asked
bodies to stay awhile under the blanched tree
branches way out in the plain, where a run of the sun,
naked, stood still, and not a sound was made and your heart
shuddered, I close my eyes; I have bridled my whole heart.

                                            Yesterday's rain
              and the water still in hoof prints.

STABAT MATER

The backs of hills are brackened, felt-
brown as the fallow deer, a pelt

tufted crust. Shallow, blackened
night quickens to attraction.

Each mound begs passage via vicissitude;
the light hangs itself on a narcissus-blue

line, like God asserting presence
in even the minim-essence.

As if to say, a gain
is a measure is a slack of skein

and again, I say unto you,
it is easier for light to pass through

the eye of a needle. For lack
of heart I pluck lilac,

watch the imminence of matter
matter. Each pap an altar

of ravines of gorse;
I prick a finger gorged

on claret. Off course everything is
insistent of itself; a concordance this

crown of thorns. The rain alters shape
according to must, hills, agape

where the hills meet a V,
a cervix, the length a neck of geese

I watch. The cervus bow their heads in matrimony
in service of coarse sanctimony.

O sacred hart I seek
to hold the wind meekly

like the sky through your velvet-horns,
like the scorned woman reborn.

GLESGA PRAYER

Our Father who art in heaven, I am in love.
Again. For which I offer thanks.
Tonight, I step in dog shit. I don't care.
I thank God for it. I ought to start with praise,
but praise is hard for me. Did I tell you
about the boy who taught me how to pray?
He always starts with praise. I see him from time
to time. Do you? Once at the train station
I said I want to have dinner with you. He said I want to eat
with you, I want to eat on you, I want to eat you!
Take care of him.

Now, confession—the worst part. At night
the fox crosses the street to eat from a bin.
He looks like a tired-faced woman except
he is beautiful. I'm sorry for the times I've stayed
out in short long rain. Soft with dew, I look
like a small puddle. And in my loneliness and fear
I've thought create in me a clean heart O God.
Forgive me. This is my favourite sin: despair—
whose lust I celebrate with love and prayer.

Heavenly Father, thank you for this greasy, delicious
mince pie and this fish supper (though
it's made me kind of sick). Also thanks
for this Irn-Bru, so sweet and so cold.
At the gardens last week, I sat and watched
two boys blowing up johnnies. I could have
let it mean anything but was moved again
by how little we ask for. Two mums pushed
their children in the opposite direction.
I laughed and got a dirty look. Dear Lord,
we move with love from metaphor to metaphor,
which is—let it be so—a kind of prayer.

I'm usually asleep by now. I won't bother you
with requests. Though keep the one I love safe.
Perhaps even a little bit of money my way…
This city is perched on the skyline like dirty doves.
It makes me think sometimes of you. What makes me
think of me is the poor soul who swims out
too far and then looks back to land. Ahead, he sees
eternity, and suddenly his arms no longer work,
and down he goes. As I fall fast, remember me.

THE LOVES OF PLANTS

*I don't remember my first brush with pollen, yet I've
watched words flower sideways across your mouth.*
   —Elizabeth Willis

These stems are trembling, I pluck them
up. I have /ˈdʌbəljuː/'s rattling
in my mouth, the wind is
what caused them to bloom
a forsaken flower, the blood
of its dead lover. They cling too
closely to my tongue, stammering the stem
of the thing. The word is clanking:
anemone, anemone, anemone.

GLOSSARY

ANEMONE
see 21, 27, 38, 62, 75

I. Ovid's *Metamorphoses*, otherwise known as *The Book of Transformations*, recalls the plant created by Venus's tears, when she wept nectar onto the blood of her dead lover, Adonis. At its touch, the blood swelled up, as foam from the sea. In less than an hour, a flower was created like a pomegranate. Enjoyment of the anemone is brief; like seeds of a rind, the winds deflower it.

II. In Greek, the word 'anemone' derives from *anemos*, meaning 'wind', though its feminine suffix gives the additional meaning of 'daughter of the wind'. According to etymologists, the word has close ties to *anima*: 'rational soul', 'desire', 'spirit'. The spoken word becomes the breath of life.

III. When Asa Gray, a nineteenth-century American botanist, began writing his *Manual of the Botany of the Northern United States, from New England to Wisconsin and South to Ohio and Pennsylvania Inclusive*, he reflected that the flower got its name from the belief that it only opened when the wind blew.

IV. When Ruskin would visit Coniston during the summer months, he enjoyed a botany lesson followed by a good tea. It was in his nature to recover from a heartbreak there, often taking the air and 'having fine talks with the anemones, in their tongue'. (What language were they speaking?) When recalling a particular excursion to Florence, he mentioned the anemone's 'exquisitely nervous trembling and veining colour—violin playing in scarlet on white ground'. Later in life, his metaphor for love became 'leaves that grow among the ruins'.[1]

V. In H.D.'s aphoristic *Notes on Thought and Vision*, the anemone becomes a sea-flower, possessing a rare and transmutable force: 'That over-mind seems a cap, like water, transparent, fluid yet with definite body, contained in a definite space. It is like a closed sea-plant, or anemone. Into that over-mind, thoughts pass and are visible like fish swimming

---

[1] John Ruskin, *Letters of John Ruskin to Bernard Quaritch 1867–1888*, ed. by Charlotte Quaritch Wrentmore (London: Bernard Quaritch, 1938), p. 80; John Ruskin, *The Brantwood Diary of John Ruskin*, ed. by Helen Viljoen (New Haven, CT: Yale University Press, 1971), p. 383; John Ruskin, *The Letters of John Ruskin to Lord and Lady Mount-Temple*, ed. by John Lewis Bradley (Columbus, OH: Ohio State University Press, 1964), p. 197.

under clear water.'² The anemone indeed possesses *anima* in this instance, in the Jungian sense, where osmosis yields the transcendent, and the anemone's feelers become nerves of the brain.

---

² H.D., *Notes on Thought and Vision* (San Francisco, CA: City Lights Publishing, 1982), p. 19.

BLUEBELL
see 19, 40, 65, 69

I. Bluebells used to be known as hyacinths, and the French still call them *jacinthes des bois*.

II. The *Hyacinthoides non-scripta* was first described by Carl Linnaeus in his pivotal work, *Species Plantarum* (1753), where the specified epithet *non-scripta* means 'unlettered'. As a 'primordial' hyacinth, Linnaeus wanted to differentiate this particular plant from the classical hyacinth of Greek mythology. The flower was originally given the name bluebell because, unlike other hyacinths then known, it lacked the formation of the letters A, I, A, I in its petals (alas), which was evidently distinguishable on the petals of other hyacinths.

III. The mythical flower, which is almost certainly not the modern hyacinth, blossomed from the blood of the dying prince Hyacinthus. His lover, Apollo, shed tears on the newly formed flower, marking its petals in the shapes of A, I, A, I (woe! woe!) to commemorate his grief. In strict botanical taxonomy the flower is one of the Scilloideae.

IV. Keats called the flower 'sapphire Queen of the Mid-May'.[3] The bluebell is also common in Scotland:

> Binna feart, hinny,
> yin day we'll gang thegither
> tae thae stourie
> blaebellwids,
> and loss wirsels —[4]

---

[3] John Keats, 'Fancy', *The Complete Poems* (London: Penguin, 1977), p. 307.
[4] Kathleen Jamie, 'Speirin', *The Tree House* (London: Picador, 2004), p. 14.

CANNA
see 16, 23, 34, 41, 44, 50, 58, 64, 70

I. Sometimes known as the Canna Lily, though not a true lily in the slightest, the closest living relations to the tropical perennial are the plant families Zingiberaceae and Musaceae, gingers and bananas respectively.

II. From the Latin meaning 'cane' or 'reed', though the Scottish island bears the same name presumably from the Norse for 'knee-shaped'. Earlier Indo-European origins suggest 'bend' as a possible root. (The walking stick is born.)

III. Wallace Stevens is a botanist in 'Anecdote of Canna'. As in science, here the initial poetic act is to observe:

> Huge are the canna in the dreams of
> X, the mighty thought, the mighty man. [...]

From the Greek *anekdota*, to mean 'unpublished', the poem, too, has an unfinished quality about it. (Are we imagining an imagined canna, or a real one?—See this nine-lined poem in its entirety.) The flower's re-representation brings into question its translatability. Make enough copies and the original is lost. Yet note the immense size of the canna in dreams. Its presence is overwhelming and its insistence on this 'fact' is emphasized. But for Stevens, things as we see them in reality may not be accurately depicted in our imagination. The canna seems as large as the philosophical concepts 'thought' and 'man', filling the terrace, filling the Capitol buildings, filling the mind. Neither parable nor anecdote, the poem mixes fact and fiction, resulting in fragmented thoughts. This can be seen not only in the use of ellipses but also in the use of 'X'. The letter becomes an exercise in semiotics: insert 'the poet', the Greek symbol, an abbreviation for Christ, the bands that form Plato's *anima mundi*, chiasmus, a plant structure. Which Stevens intends for us is not known, nor the chasms of the imagination.

The inevitable day-break disrupts what Stevens refers to as 'somnambulism' in the poem (or sleepwalking).[5] What remains is the canna, the central image of the poem, because for Stevens, the flower is

---

[5] See James Longenbach, *Wallace Stevens: The Plain Sense of Things* (Oxford: Oxford University Press, 1991), p. 61

fact, 'the exquisite environment of fact'.[6] The canna is tangible, unlike the realm of dreams. And it is definite. We are drawn to the flower in both dream and reality, yet it is only through continual observation of the flower in the waking world that we can verify and validate our thoughts in relationship to other 'thought[s] | Or thing[s]'. Stevens is right; if we slept forever, we would indeed never know another thought or thing. Our point of reference, the living world, would be closed off to us.

The canna conflates the fact of bodily existence—the fact of being 'in bloom'—and an Aristotelian artistic position: art reflects life. A horticultural act is aligned with a human act insomuch that the canna will live and die, too. If we observe long enough, we can watch it happen. And for Stevens, poetry, like the canna, exists in the real: 'Poetry has to be something more than a conception of the mind. It has to be a revelation of nature. Conceptions are artificial. Perceptions are essential.'[7] That is to say, poetry reveals something of our nature in nature.

---

[6] *Adagia*, in *Complete Poetry and Prose*, p. 904.

[7] *Adagia*, in *Complete Poetry and Prose*, p. 904.

CRUCIFEROUS
see 17, 22, 24, 35, 49, 71

I. From neo-Latin, *cruciferous* means 'cross-bearing' and relates to plants of the cabbage family because its flowers have four equal petals arranged crosswise.

II. H.D.'s *Trilogy* is a step towards mystical enlightenment. To achieve such transcendence, one must comprehend the symbol. Trees in *The Flowering of the Rod* allude to the rod of Caduceus, Aaron's rod, and the flowering rood: the Cross. But we must go back to the beginning.

The Paradisal Garden bore (at least) two trees: the Tree of Divine Life, and the Tree of the knowledge of good and evil. The aboriginal couple seemed not to know that to eat the fruit of the latter would be to bring evil into the world: and yet the clue is in the name of the tree. One cannot know what evil is if only good exists. *For God doth know*, said the serpent, *that in the day ye eate thereof, then your eyes shal bee opened: and yee shall bee as Gods, knowing good and euill* (Genesis 3:5). What slippery use of the word 'knowing', in Hebrew יָדַע. Cf. Genesis 4:1: *And Adam knew Eue his wife.* The tree of language was already rotten at the roots. Language was fallen before the Fall.

The Tree of Divine Life was replanted on 'The-place-of-a-skull' (*Tribute to the Angels* 2).[8]

In *The Flowering of the Rod* 19, the mysterious Lady sets 'a charred tree before us, | burnt and stricken to the heart; | was it may-tree or apple?' The may-tree, the hawthorn, was once a symbol of resurrection. In Gaelic folklore the plant was said to heal the broken heart. Yet H.D. presents the tree itself as 'stricken to the heart'. Even doctors fall ill. As Marianne Moore wrote, 'All are | naked, none is safe'.[9] Everything created is susceptible to corruption. Such is the effect of consumption from a tree of dubious fruit, a tree 'sealed with the seal of death'.

The tree is burnt but not dead. Is this instrument of man's first mistake apple or may-tree? Is it the outward sign of death or, transfigured to the Rood, the hidden sign of life-in-death?

There or not-there, we see the tree flowering.

---

[8] All references to H.D.'s *Trilogy* are in the main body of the text and refer to the Carcanet edition (Manchester: Carcanet, 1973).

[9] Marianne Moore, 'What Are Years?', *Complete Poems* (London: Faber and Faber, 1984), p. 95.

III.

> we crossed the charred portico,
> [...]
> entered a shrine; like a ghost,
> [...]
> we saw the tree flowering;
> [...]

The portico is the temple's porch, the façade outside the entrance to the sacred place. We enter this poem, the twentieth in H.D.'s *Tribute to the Angels*, as though entering a church. The poem is a church is a garden-square. *The Walls Do Not Fall* takes place both in ancient Egypt and Second-World-War London; analogously, this poem is both medieval Catholic church and Greek temple, 'house' and 'shrine'. The flowers of one bloom in the garden of the other.

The poem's just visible, just divisible stanzas remind one of the cruciform floor plan of a church. In one sense, the poem is a journey through this cruciform space, which itself represents the journey of Christ: from the vestibule (in which He is baptized with the coming-near 'Spirit' and 'passed through a flame—doorless') through the nave (where He is found among the peregrinating people, the 'we' that appears in almost every stanza in the body of the poem) to the sanctuary (the place of His sacrifice on the 'ordinary tree'). By travelling to this tree, the poem dares to 'approach the high-altar'.

The burning sin in the garden is still present here. Even the temple's portico is 'charred'. See also the blackened seed of that word from Genesis: 'knowing'. The irony of the knowledge of good and evil is that we find ourselves 'still not knowing' whether we are 'there or not-there'. Though physically present in the place of worship, one may or may not be truly 'there' in the Church. Schrödinger himself would not have admitted the possibility of being both. We move between seed-bed and stony ground in this earthly garden, never entirely sure of our condition, and never at home. While one stanza goes 'through a wall' with a semicolon, the poem's rooms have unstable walls, like '(like the wall)', which closes its stanza on a curved bracket.

But the poem hesitantly moves forward, and finds the tree, in its sanctuary, flowering. In the final stanza the attention has been transferred from 'we' to 'it'. The direction of the poem—a single sentence, like every other in *Trilogy*—is towards this tree, which 'bears healing', which 'brings life to the living' (*The Walls Do Not Fall* 3). The cruciform church traditionally faces east, where the sun rises. One enters, 'like a ghost', in the west, where the sun sets, in the 'not knowing' of darkness. Inside, one faces the immanent light. This extraordinary tree is ordinary in that it could not flower if it were not in the east.

Apocalypse is as near as Genesis. The city-garden of its twenty-first chapter, the new earth it describes, is 'an old garden-square' made new: *Et civitas in quadro posita est*. And the city lieth foure square. (Again, the leaves of cruciferous plants are four-square.)

See also, in the last chapter of that last book, *lignum vitae*, the tree of life, burnt, broken, renewed, whose leaves are *ad sanitatem gentium*, for the healing of the nations.

(*The Walls Do Not Fall* 25: 'the Kingdom is a Tree'.)

CRYPTOGAMAE
see 19, 27, 34, 41

I. Linnaeus approaches nomenclature halfway between poet and scientist; he classified between types of florescence, or flowering, by whether it was public, visible to the eye, or clandestine, invisible to the naked eye. In the plant kingdom, clandestine marriages included the (scarcely visible) flowerings of moss, ferns, and fungi. The word cryptogamae itself comes from the Greek *kryptos*, meaning 'hidden', and *gameein*, 'to marry', a kind of Shakespearean evocation seen in the clandestine promiscuity of characters in the woods of *A Midsummer Night's Dream*. A connection between flowering and sexuality is drawn. The nectar from Oberon's 'little western flower' elicits love at first sight, a prelude to a play of triple weddings. The moss and ferns of the wood provide the background, perhaps even a bed, for Helena or Titania. Lines from Pyramus suggest as much: 'O wherefore, nature, didst thou lions frame? | Since lion vile hath here deflow'red my dear'.[10] One cannot ignore, especially in this context, the resemblance of 'deflow'red' to 'devoured'.

II. In *The Purpose of Playing*, Louis Montrose emphasizes the connection between Cupid's 'juice', or 'love-in-idleness', and sexuality in *A Midsummer Night's Dream*: the shedding of menstrual blood and the blood shed by virgins.[11] Such an austere physicality, blood, becomes the visible manifestation of the invisible biology of a woman, as seen in *Light Iris*, an oil on canvas by Georgia O'Keeffe.[12]

III. Famously, when asked about the influence of Linnaeus on his own work, Goethe replied, 'With the exception of Shakespeare and Spinoza, I know no one among the no longer living who has influenced me more strongly'.[13] For proof, see his *Metamorphosis of Plants* (1790) and most of his poetry. It is clear that Goethe had already arrived at the homologous

---

[10] William Shakespeare, *A Midsummer Night's Dream*, 5.1.289–90, *The Complete Signet Classic Shakespeare*, ed. by Sylvan Barnet (New York, NY: Harcourt Brace Jovanovich, 1972), p. 553.

[11] Louis Montrose, *The Purpose of Playing: Shakespeare and the Cultural Politics of the Elizabethan Theatre* (Chicago: The University of Chicago Press, 1996), p. 174. See also *A Midsummer Night's Dream*, 2.1.168.

[12] See poem on the same, *supra*.

[13] Cited in Roland Moberg, 'What People Have Said about Linnaeus' <http://www.linnaeus.uu.se/online/life/8_3.html> [accessed 28 April 2015].

nature of leaf organs in plants, from cotyledons to photosynthetic leaves, fifty years before Richard Owen, a *Dinosauria* himself, and a staunch opponent of Darwin.

IV. The bioluminescence of the sea is the sea in bloom, a phenomenon witnessed by Linnaeus and attributed to microscopic bacteria. Jules Verne notes the effect in his *Twenty Thousand Leagues Under the Sea* in his description of sailing through an ocean of milk.[14]

V. For some, including W. Whitman Bailey, 'No division of the vegetable kingdom has attracted more deserved attention than that of the seaweeds or sea-mosses'. To the best of his recollection, collecting specimens involved visits to romantic cliffs and hidden caves, even venturing into the deep sea itself. 'A spice of danger does not deter the heroic algologist', says Bailey. 'Even many ladies have been successful gatherers of seaweeds.'[15] The plants do not need to be studied to be enjoyed, though he agrees it is always pleasanter to know something of the habits, uses, and even names of the objects which one treasures.

VI. 'We have lingered in the chambers of the sea | By sea-girls wreathed with seaweed red and brown | Till human voices wake us, and we drown.'[16] A debt to Longfellow's 'Seaweed', the obscured depths of ocean entangle one like hair, each strand pulling with invisible force.

---

[14] Jules Verne, *Twenty Thousand Leagues Under the Sea* (New York: Scholastic, 2000), pp. 209–10.

[15] William Whitman Bailey, 'On the Subject of Algæ', in *The Botanical Collector's Handbook* (Salem, MA: G. A. Bates, 1881), pp. 46–47.

[16] T. S. Eliot, 'The Love Song of J. Alfred Prufrock', in *Collected Poems 1909–1962* (London: Faber and Faber, 2002), p. 7.

DEFINITION
see 38, 39, 41, 45, 53, 60, 66

I. Ian Hamilton Finlay's *Little Sparta* is a series of aesthetic propositions. Follow a stream one way and it becomes a pond. Approach the same stream from the opposite direction and it disappears. For Finlay, gardening is idyllic insomuch that utopia has many interpretations and yet only one meaning.

II. A stile connects a tamer garden with a wilder ridge. Three inscriptions are presented along a stony footpath:

> THESIS *fence*
> ANTITHESIS *gate*
> SYNTHESIS *stile*

III. Juxtaposition and definition are intrinsic to Finlay's work. 'The apparent precision and conciseness of a definition,' writes Jessie Sheeler, 'is brought to bear in ways which reveal unexpected aspects of the objects they describe and often dissolve the accepted meaning of terms, or interpretation of their reference in the 'real' world.'[17]

---

[17] Jessie Sheeler, *Little Sparta: The Garden of Ian Hamilton Finlay* (London: Frances Lincoln Publishers, 2003), cited in Philip Robinson (ed.), *The Faber Book of Gardens* (London: Faber and Faber, 2007), p. 370.

EDEN
see 13, 14, 19, 22, 29, 38, 43, 59, 69, 75

I. 'For all of its magnificent unity', writes Thomas Kranadis, '*Paradise Lost* is not monolithic. Variety coexists with decorum.'[18] So it is in any garden, in any florilegium. The garden is a unity rather than a singularity. As Milton writes in the *Tetrachordon*, 'Loneliness is the first thing which God's eye named not good.'[19] A garden cannot be understood synecdochically, looking only at one part and presuming on the whole; it must be comprehended in its varied entirety, taking account of every part and its relation to every other. Milton's Eden comprises more than one flower. Towards the end of Book IV of *Paradise Lost*, the 'blissful bower' in which the first couple will consummate their love is described:

> it was a place
> Chos'n by the sovran Planter, when he framed
> All things to mans delightful use; the roofe
> Of thickest covert was inwoven shade
> Laurel and Mirtle, and what higher grew
> Of firm and fragrant leaf; on either side
> *Acanthus*, and each odorous bushie shrub,
> Fenc'd up the verdant wall; each beauteous flour,
> *Iris* all hues, Roses, and Gessamin,
> Rear'd high their flourisht heads between, and wrought
> Mosaic; underfoot the Violet,
> Crocus, and Hyacinth with rich inlay
> Broiderd the ground [...]
>   Here in close recess
> With Flowers, Garlands, and sweet-smelling Herbs,
> Espoused *Eve* deckt first her nuptial Bed [...][20]

Everything speaks of intertwining: the flowers are a mosaic, embroidering the earth 'with rich inlay'; the roof's leaves are 'inwoven'. In the abundant garden of Milton's blank verse, flowers of rhetoric, flowers of rhythm, can

---

[18] Thomas Kranadis, 'Adam and Eve in the Garden: A Study of *Paradise Lost*, Book V', *Studies in English Literature, 1500–1900*, 4 (1964), 71–83 (p. 71).

[19] John Milton, *Tetrachordon*, in *The Works of John Milton*, ed. by Frank Allen Patterson et al., 18 vols (New York, NY: Columbia University Press, 1931–1940), IV, p. 83.

[20] John Milton, *Paradise Lost* (London: S. Simmons, 1674), pp. 105–106.

be the names of real flowers on the meandering stems of iambic lines. There is a clear sense of descent: the eye is taken from the roof of the bower, down its walls, to the ground. It is a leisurely descent, not decadent but innocently indulgent. There are small aural echoes, but, except the inoffensive 'firm and fragrant', no heavy alliterations or assonances: even the sounds in this poetic garden are balanced, moderate. Milton scatters widely his seeds of sound; every phoneme has its place.

Each flower, each word, is not only made complete by the others, but made more beautiful: *tamen bona etiam singula*, St Augustine writes, with Genesis 1:31 in mind; *simul vero universa valde bona, quia ex omnibus consistit universitatis admirabilis pulchritudo.*[21] Only the sum of created things does God deem 'very good'.

'Here in close recess': the word 'recess', with its back turned to the line's edge, evokes the slow journey of Adam and Eve to their bed. One can almost see Eve taking Adam's hand, her own back turned, into the bower, uttering the three previous words as an invitation: 'Here: in close'.

The emphasis is on relationality. Man is incomplete without woman. A flower is incomplete without a stem. God Himself is a Trinity, a relationship of three Persons. From this model, human life and gardens alike exist intradependently. They live by reciprocity.

It is in Book IX, when Adam, for the first time, is not by Eve's side, when the flower is removed from the stem, that corruption ensues:

> Carnation, Purple, Azure, or spect with Gold,
> Hung drooping unsustaind, them she upstaies
> Gently with Mirtle band, mindless the while,
> Her self, though fairest unsupported Flour,
> From her best prop so farr, and storm so nigh.[22]

Instead of blooming all around Eve, encompassing her and her husband, now the garden is held in her hand; and she finds it cannot sustain itself. Nor can she sustain herself alone: now she needs Adam as he, among the beasts, needed her. She is the true 'unsupported Flour', the poem outside the florilegium. She is already exiled.

---

[21] 'Each single thing is good; and taken as a whole, they are very good, because together they constitute a universe of admirable beauty.' Augustine, *Enchridion*, in *De doctrina christiana libri quatuor* (Wellesley, MA: Wellesley College Library, 1838), p. 172.

[22] Milton, *Paradise Lost*, pp. 226–27.

II.   To be rehabilitated into Eden would be an *exile* for us.
              —Ian Hamilton Finlay[23]

References to Eden in Ian Hamilton Finlay's garden, Little Sparta, are sparse and subtle. In an area of Little Sparta named the Temple Pool Garden, a stone tablet hangs from a tree. It is inscribed with a monogram: two majuscule letters, A and D, the latter under the former as though sheltered by it. Art historians might recognize the signature: a similar tablet hangs from a tree in Eden in a painting by A.D.: Albrecht Dürer. Especially near the end of his life, Dürer was fascinated by the notion of the ideal human form. His first Adam and Eve, in a copper engraving of 1504, are proportioned and positioned sculpturally; although their muscles are prominent and flexed, they do not appear to be moving. They are, like the monogram in stone, fixed emblems, fixed in the history of humanity. Eve's hand rests on an apple, mysteriously growing on what appears to be a fig tree. The couple's heads are artificially turned towards each other, suggesting that they are almost (though not sufficiently) aware of the gargantuan consequence of their decision: this is the last preternatural moment, the final innocence. The tranquil animals around them, which symbolize the four humours, or temperaments, are about to be sprung loose by the Fall. The garden will grow wild around the stone. The two figures copy each other, both standing in classical *contrapposto*, the weight of the body on one foot. Such perfect harmonies of proportion will presently be interrupted. The garden of order is one pull of a branch away from becoming a jungle.

The tablet hanging in Finlay's garden is the mark of the past: the sign of Dürer's influence, but also the stain of Eden. Most *cartellini*, fictive carriers of inscriptions in art, reveal the author's name; Finlay's modestly reveals Dürer's name—and perhaps even, if AD is another kind of abbreviation, Adam's.

Elsewhere in the Temple Pool Garden, a stone reads: 'HIC IACET | PARVULUM | QUODDAM | EX AQUA | LONGIORE | EXCERPTUM' ('Here lies a small excerpt from a longer water'). 'Here lies' indicates that the marker is a gravestone, but it refers to life-giving water. The Temple Pool, a small section of Little Sparta's water, a smaller section of the world's water, may be an excerpt, but it is a suggestive one. One reads in this water the water beyond it. One reads in Little Sparta an excerpt of the garden's history, which is an excerpt of human history, and which comprehends

---

[23] 'Detached Sentences on Exile', *Ian Hamilton Finlay: Selections*, ed. by Alec Finlay (Berkeley, CA: University of California Press, 2012), p. 188.

even the aboriginal dwelling-place from which humanity is irrevocably exiled.

III. Emily Dickinson would have understood. Her own two-acre garden was her 'little bit of Eden', wherein she herself was Eve.[24] Finlay writes that to be rehabilitated into Eden would be an exile; Dickinson, for whom a regenerated Eden, a Paradise regained, was a real possibility, recognizes nonetheless that such a place could be overwhelmingly unfamiliar:

> Come slowly—Eden!
> Lips unused to Thee—
> Bashful—sip thy Jessamines—
> As the fainting Bee—
>
> Reaching late his flower,
> Round her chamber hums—
> Counts his nectars—
> Enters—and is lost in Balms.[25]

There is so much to do in Paradise; and yet everything one can do is replete with pleasure, so that to do just one thing, as in this poem, more than suffices. And even this one thing—sipping the nectar of jasmines—is too much. What chance does mere man have when the bee, for whom drinking nectar is a quotidian enterprise, faints and 'is lost' in tranquilized ecstasy?

Eden, for Dickinson, symbolizes pleasure: pleasure that is licit but sensually engulfing; pleasure about which there is something always just out of reach. Here, the implications of sexual desire are striking. The flower is female, the bee male; in the reciprocity of their bond, the flower seems to belong to the bee, and in the end, the opposite appears to be true. It is 'his flower', but 'her chamber'. But the 'Balms' in which he is lost belong to neither. They are the pleasures of Eden, of unbridled life.

The opening line, 'Come slowly—Eden!', itself comes slowly, with heavy, languorous stresses. The air of Eden is immediately intoxicating. The brief pauses of Dickinson's dashes are supplemented in the fifth line by a different pause, perhaps a longer one, with a punctuation mark altogether more unusual for the poet: the comma. It comes in the midst

---

[24] *The Letters of Emily Dickinson*, ed. by Thomas H. Johnson (Cambridge, MA: The Belknap Press of Harvard University Press, 1958), LL 59, 9.

[25] *The Poems of Emily Dickinson*, ed. by R. W. Franklin (Cambridge, MA: The Belknap Press of Harvard University Press, 1999), F 205.

of a lingering moment of anticipation, before the bee at last devours its food. In contrast with 'Thee' and 'Bee', the second stanza's 'hums' is followed by the pararhyme 'Balms', whose vowel sound occurs nowhere else in the poem: the fulfilment of expectation comes in this last word, and it is something entirely new and unexpected, the most pleasant of surprises.

'Expulsion from Eden grows indistinct in the presence of flowers so blissful, and with no disrespect to Genesis, Paradise remains': Dickinson enclosed this note in a bouquet she gave to a new neighbour in 1878.[26] Paradise remains: Eden is 'alive' to Dickinson.[27] New life is so excessively good that it eclipses corruption.

For Dickinson, the revivification of her flowers in spring was the only viable reason to believe in the Resurrection. Unlike Milton, whom she called 'the great florist', Dickinson felt that there was no need to regain Paradise; whether it was ever truly lost was dubious.[28] Still, her Eden draws deeply from Milton's. The 'Jessamines' of this poem recall the jessamine in Book IV of *Paradise Lost*, quoted above; others mentioned in the same passage, including the rose and the violet, make frequent and important appearances in Dickinson. The difference is that Milton's Eden is a thing of legend, and Dickinson's is outside her door.

How can this be? If the world is no longer Eden, what was Emily Dickinson experiencing? Is it that the external garden has a correlative, a fulfilling antitype, existing within the observer? Northrop Frye, reading Milton, offers this idea: 'There is a garden inside the human mind, walled up and guarded by angels still, yet a place that the Word of God can open'.[29]

A mind so cultivated is a new Eden. Adam and Eve, though fallen, retain the image and likeness of God, as the flower retains its sweetness. Upon Adam's vow, at the conclusion of *Paradise Lost*, to acknowledge God thenceforth in love and fear, the Archangel Michael advises him to garden his soul, planting the virtues: patience, temperance, and, centrally, love:

---

[26] *The Letters of Emily Dickinson*, L 552.

[27] And, for Dickinson, 'the Alive' is what matters. See *The Letters of Emily Dickinson*, LL 233, 260, 1045; and Judith Farr and Louise Carter, *The Gardens of Emily Dickinson* (Cambridge, MA: Harvard University Press, 2004), p. 179.

[28] *The Letters of Emily Dickinson*, L 1038.

[29] Northrop Frye, *Five Essays on Milton's Epics* (Toronto, ON: University of Toronto Press, 1965), p. 58.

> then wilt thou not be loath
> To leave this Paradise, but shalt possess
> A paradise within thee, happier farr.[30]

Happier far: far from the garden in body, Adam is to grow and to savor spiritual blossoms. Though he hears 'happier' from the Archangel, one might imagine Adam here instead as Coleridge's mariner: a sadder and a wiser man. A kind of oxymoron occurs in the final words of Milton's poem: 'thir solitarie way'.[31] The reciprocity of human life is changed. The way is shared but solitary.

What Adam and Eve—what humanity—must do now, in Milton's understanding, remains as before the Fall: to seek God in the garden. But now the garden is an interior place, in which the weather is less certain, in which the weeds are more pernicious; and into which one must look alone.

From their own bodies the souls of the dead are exiled.

IV. The Tree of Life has often been read as a prefiguration of the Cross. Its blossom is blood.

Sapience and *savor* have the same root. Taste and see.

---

[30] Milton, *Paradise Lost*, p. 331.

[31] Milton, *Paradise Lost*, p. 333.

GOD
see 13, 14, 16, 33, 34, 40, 41, 43, 44, 45, 49, 50, 55, 56, 60, 63, 65, 66, 70, 71, 73

I. The Gardener's voice was heard as He walked in the cool of the day.

HIBISCUS
see 17, 59

I. *Hibiscus mutabilis*, or the 'blushing hibiscus': a shrub that behaves like a northern perennial; the flowers, when in bloom, turn white in the morning, pink by noon, and red in the evening, all within the same day. The flower will bloom regardless of spectacle. The prize relies on seeing.

II. In ancient China, the *Hibiscus mutabilis* was believed to resemble beautiful ladies. A Chinese proverb runs: 'Cotton rose-mallow out of the water' (出水芙蓉). It is used to describe a young lady of appreciated beauty. There exists a certain number of historical paintings depicting beautiful young women titled *Hibiscus mutabilis*, noted for the delicacy and intricacy of brushstrokes.

III. On the phenomenon of the blushing hibiscus, the most immediate questions are *how?* and *why?* One could examine the molecular biology of the plant, attributing its blush to a rise in temperature, or even cite its Darwinist strategy for survival. But a contradiction remains. As M. M. Mahood describes, the colour change is a sign of senescence; it heralds the death of the flower.[32]

IV. On January 31, 1921, D. H. Lawrence wrote 'Hibiscus and Salvia Flowers', an urgent attack on Italian socialism. His use of a botanical vernacular throughout the poem becomes emblematic of the noise of revolutionaries, and of what he sees as disparities between artificial order and natural order:

> Rose-red, princess hibiscus, rolling her pointed Chinese petals!
> Azalea and camellia, single peony
> And pomegranate bloom and scarlet mallow-flower
> And all the eastern, exquisite royal plants
> That noble blood has brought us down the ages!
> Gently nurtured, frail and splendid
> > Hibiscus flower –
> Alas, the Sunday coats of Sicilian bolshevists![33]

---

[32] M.M. Mahood, *The Poet as Botanist* (Cambridge: Cambridge University Press, 2008), p. 2.

[33] D. H. Lawrence, 'Hibiscus and Salvia Flowers', *Birds, Beasts and Flowers* (London: Martin Secker, 1923), p. 64 (pp. 62–69).

The flowers, refined after years of cultivating, are now distant relatives of their natural, unruly selves. The hibiscus, a princess, has become royal, 'gently nurtured' and of 'royal blood', an amalgamation of an organic and an aristocratic existence. There is something of primitivism in this exoticizing of the east; yet Lawrence is also drawing comparisons with more familiar phenomena: 'Rose of the oldest races of princesses, Polynesian | Hibiscus'. Gauguin's influence cannot be overlooked, as his depictions of Polynesian royalty present a similar juxtaposition of the natural world with ideas of aristocracy, the West confronted by the East (or by a Westerner's image of the East).

Gauguin's painting *Arii Matamoe*, or 'The Royal End', depicts the severed head of the Tahitian King Pōmare V, surrounded by flowers and mourning women. The head is presented on a platter ritualistically, recalling the decapitations of Orpheus and John the Baptist. The red hibiscus, a Malaysian symbol for currency, is scattered throughout the painting.

D. H. Lawrence read Gauguin's *Noa Noa*, an illustrated collage of Tahiti, six months prior to composing 'Hibiscus and Salvia Flowers'. The book was written as a means of escaping 'everything that is artificial and conventional', according to its author.[34] Lawrence took this concept and applied it to this poem: the socialists in the poem are outside their hotel, and, as suggested by their association with Polynesian flowers, outside European civilization. Lawrence was fond of neither the socialists nor European civilization; what he desired was the hibiscus in its perfect autonomy.

---

[34] Cited in Nancy Mowll Mathews, *Paul Gauguin: An Erotic Life* (New Haven, CT: Yale University Press, 2001), p. 167.

HONEY
see 19, 24, 33, 35, 36, 39, 40, 49, 50

I. It is debated among theological scholars what might constitute the wildness of John the Baptist's wild honey, as referred to in Matthew 3:4 and Mark 1:6. It is possible that the honey was only nominally honey and did not come from bees at all. First-century Palestinian apiculture was famously undeveloped.

II. Wildness is not necessarily madness, but the theologians have failed to note that wild honey might be the same as mad honey, that is, honey containing grayanotoxins (so called after the Japanese species *Leucothoe grayana*, in turn named after Asa Gray (see 'Anemone', III, *supra*)). The presence of grayanotoxins in honey, most commonly found in the nectar of rhododendrons, can render it poisonous to humans. The nectar of *Andromeda polifolia* produces a honey that, when ingested by humans, is paralysing, sometimes fatally so.

III.   Nothing worth noting
       except an Andromeda [...]

These are the first two lines of Lorine Niedecker's 'Linnaeus in Lapland'.[35] The form—five-line stanzas in which the shorter fourth line rhymes with the third—is Niedecker's, though she admits the 'influence of haiku I suppose'.[36]

The 'Andromeda' in the second line is *Andromeda polifolia*, named by Linnaeus on his expedition to Lapland in 1732. One can suppose the species seemed to him stripped bare in its harsh surroundings, like the Andromeda of Greek myth. Niedecker notes the 'Nothing worth noting' as Linnaeus himself would have. She sees herself in his role, the roving observer and namer of things, quiet interpreter of nature.

The 'quadrangular', lanceolate leaves of the *Andromeda* seem to attach it immediately, in the mind of Niedecker's Linnaeus, to the native people: the plant's 'shoots' are rhymed quickly with the people's 'boots'. Both constitute foundations of life. In the second stanza the rhyme is

---

[35] Lorine Niedecker, *Collected Works*, ed. by Jenny Penberthy (Berkeley, CA: University of California Press, 2002), p. 181.

[36] Lorine Niedecker, *Niedecker and the Correspondence with Zukofsky, 1931–1970*, ed. by Jenny Penberthy (Cambridge: Cambridge University Press, 1993), p. 230.

subtler, more oblique: the 'blossoms' are twinned with 'bosoms', though the bosoms are those of leaves, not of the people. By this point in the poem, the plants and the people are successfully confused. Note the final lines of each stanza: 'of the people'; 'of the leaves'.

The 'leaves' of the Bible, of course, would be held at the 'bosoms' of those who must 'swim | to church'. They might be there to avoid being 'taxed'. This seems a curious thing to include in the poem. But it suggests a remarkable doggedness. Andromeda herself had to demonstrate nothing less (not to mention the plant). What is striking about the people's journey 'thru the floods' to church is their hardiness, their hardness. This has a beauty of its own, and is why Niedecker's next image is of 'blossoms'. They are not nameless, strengthless petals on a wet, black bough; they are stronger-bosomed things.

IV.   The Iudgements of the Lord are true, and righteous altogether.
      More to bee desired are they then gold, yea, then much fine gold:
      sweeter also then hony, and the hony combe.
                              —Psalm 19:9–10

V.   And well his words became him—was he not
      A full-cell'd honeycomb of eloquence
      Stored from all flowers?
                              —Alfred Tennyson[37]

VI.   Towards the close of his life the famous Swedish botanist
      Linnaeus took great pleasure in reading his own books and
      would cry out: 'How beautiful! What I would not give to have
      written that!'
                              —G. J. Whitrow[38]

---

[37] Alfred Tennyson, 'Edwin Morris; or The Lake', in *The Works of Alfred Lord Tennyson* (Ware: Wordsworth Poetry Library, 1994), p. 366.

[38] G. J. Whitrow, *What is Time?* (Oxford: Oxford University Press, 1972), p. 21.

IKEBANA
see 16, 33, 44, 50

I. Ikebana has something of a great painting; a sudden shift from stillness to movement, then back to stillness. There is a reason the word means *living flowers*.

II. Traditionally, Japanese floral arranging is done in silence. The stem and leaves are composed, drawing emphasis toward shape, line, frame. Much like haiku, ikebana is a creative expression with certain rules to govern its form. Both are reflexive in quality, somewhere between a self-portrait and a still life. Where haiku gives life to words, ikebana gives life to flowers.

III.   In what sense can verse, written in terms of visible hieroglyphics, be reckoned true poetry? It might seem that poetry, which like music is a *time art*, weaving its unities out of successive impressions of sound, could with difficulty assimilate a verbal medium consisting largely of semi-pictorial appeals to the eye.
—Ezra Pound[39]

IV. One can imagine ikebana like kanji characters: pictorial, compressed, understated. One stroke becomes part of a greater whole. The condensation of the objective and the direct in floral arranging and poetry intensifies the sense of beauty in a single flower, or word, similar to the Imagists' idea of isolating objects through the use of 'luminous details'.

---

[39] Ezra Pound, 'Preface', in Ernest Fenollosa and Ezra Pound, *The Chinese Written Character as a Medium for Poetry: A Critical Edition*, ed. by Haun Saussy, Jonathan Stalling, and Lucas Klein (New York, NY: Fordham University Press), p. 43.

LILY-OF-THE-VALLEY
see 27, 33, 39, 58, 63, 73

I.   As cool as the pale wet leaves
                      of lily-of-the-valley
      She lay beside me in the dawn.
                          —Ezra Pound[40]

---

[40] Ezra Pound, 'Alba', in *Imagist Poetry*, ed. by Peter Jones (London: Penguin, 2001), p. 96.

PRIMROSE
see 70

I. The evening primrose opens at night in less than a minute. Young roots can be eaten like vegetables. Note their peppery flavour. It was once known as 'king's cure-all', though it should be noted that its efficacy has not been demonstrated in clinical trials.

PROSERPINA
see 19, 38, 50, 55

I. Dante Gabriel Rossetti paints her with her left hand holding the forbidden pomegranate. The right hand is holding the left's wrist; but it is too late. There is a bite in the fruit. The exposed seeds gleam with the reflected light of the upper world, the world to which she is no longer granted access. Rossetti's sonnet, also named after her, was designed from the start to be joined with the painting, to form part of it. The 1877 version has an Italian rendition of the sonnet on the canvas, its English translation on the frame; the 1882 version has the English on the canvas. 'Afar the flowers of Enna from this drear | Dire fruit, which, tasted once, must thrall me here.'[41] Enna is the Sicilian city around which, Cicero writes, 'lacus lucique sunt plurimi atque laetissimi flores omni tempore anni' ('there are numerous lakes and copses, and flowers in profusion at all seasons').[42] The garden of Proserpina is another Eden.

II. Which brings us to Algernon Charles Swinburne. 'The Garden of Proserpine' is one of his most beautifully dreary works; his 'Hymn to Proserpine' is a grayer, more turgid lament for paganism. This latter poem is known for its dismissal of Christ—'Thou hast conquered, O pale Galilaean; the world has grown gray from thy breath'—upon which G. K. Chesterton commented, 'But when I read the same poet's accounts of paganism (as in "Atalanta"), I gathered that the world was, if possible, more gray before the Galilaean breathed on it than afterwards'.[43] Swinburne proposes that Mary, Queen of Heaven, replaced (and should be again replaced by) the Roman and pagan queen Proserpine. The poem addresses Christ:

> Not as thine, not as thine was our mother, a blossom of flowering
>   seas, [...]
> For thine came pale and a maiden, and sister to sorrow; but ours,
> Her deep hair heavily laden with odour and colour of flowers,
> White rose of the rose-white water, a silver splendour, a flame,

---

[41] D. G. Rossetti, 'Proserpine (For a Picture)', in *The Collected Works of Dante Gabriel Rossetti*, ed. by W. M. Rossetti, 2 vols (London: Ellis, 1886), I, p. 253.

[42] Marcus Tullius Cicero, *The Verrine Orations*, trans. by L. H. G. Greenwood, 2 vols (Cambridge, MA: Harvard University Press, 1928), I, XLVIII, pp. 414–15.

[43] A. C. Swinburne, *Swinburne: Selected Poetry and Prose* (New York, NY: Modern Library, 1968), p. 123; G. K. Chesterton, *Orthodoxy*, in *G. K. Chesterton: The Dover Reader* (New York: Dover, 2014), p. 321.

> Bent down to us that besought her, and earth grew sweet with her name.[44]

The description of the 'deep hair heavily laden' evokes Rossetti's Proserpina, evokes Jane Morris, Rossetti's constant model and unattainable queen (unattainable because she was William Morris's wife). The hair in the painting is as deep in colour as the seeds of the pomegranate.

The connection between the Mother of God and flowers, made in literature frequently for nearly two millenia, works naturally for Swinburne's floral 'mother'. She is reflected in nature, and nature in her, as in a pool: 'White rose of the rose-white water'. She is a 'blossom of flowering seas', whose blooms, under the surface of the myth, or of the paint, cannot be seen *en plein air*. Swinburne's queen is an illusory sea-garden, in which he plants the flowers of his own fancy.

Later, when Swinburne writes 'The Garden of Proserpine', what is 'pale' is no longer the Galilaean but the 'beds of blowing rushes | Where no leaf blooms or blushes', and even Proserpine herself: 'Pale, beyond porch and portal, | Crowned with calm leaves, she stands | Who gathers all things mortal | With cold immortal hands'. The dreamed queen has hardened into a statue. Now the speaker is 'weary of days and hours, | Blown buds of barren flowers'.[45] Swinburne luxuriates in this barrenness; it is somehow not dissimilar to the clinically pure 'rose-white water', the 'flame' of the livelier Proserpine in the 'Hymn'.

III. Swinburne's Proserpine in her garden is not only the goddess of death but the embodiment of death. She is the ultimate cold comfort. The flowers she gathers, and carries through his poems, are always flowers of mourning.

John Ruskin, writing to Swinburne, compared the man himself to a deathly flower, but in a nice way: 'I should as soon think of finding fault with you as with a thundercloud or a nightshade blossom. All I can say of you, or them—is that God made you, and that you are very wonderful and beautiful.' Later in the letter, and somewhat more peculiarly, he tells Swinburne: 'you are rose graftings set in dung'.[46] For Ruskin, the

---

[44] Swinburne, *Selected Poetry and Prose*, pp. 125–26.

[45] Swinburne, *Selected Poetry and Prose*, pp. 159–60.

[46] John Ruskin, letter to Algernon Charles Swinburne, in *The Swinburne Letters*, ed. by Cecil Y. Lang, 6 vols (New Haven: Yale University Press, 1959–62), I, p. 182. Ruskin writes about the natural phenomena and mythology of nightshades at great length in his book *The Queen of the Air*.

greatest were often the earliest stricken by root rot. He was concerned for Swinburne.

He was also concerned with Proserpine. Ruskin's Proserpine, like Rossetti's, perhaps even like Swinburne's, was personified by a real woman, though a woman so unattainable as to be unreal. Ruskin's was Rose La Touche. The name sounds fictitious; so does the life, a tragic one. (Vladimir Nabokov's *Lolita* draws much from, and alludes to, La Touche.) Rose declined Ruskin's hand in marriage, partly for her own idiosyncratic religious reasons. She was placed in a nursing home by her parents and died at the age of twenty-seven. Ruskin is thought to have gone (to a greater or lesser degree) mad afterwards.

His *Proserpina* is a book of flowers for his Rose, the greatest and earliest stricken by root rot. He wished to create a post-Linnaean taxonomical nomenclature, a 'Systema Proserpina', which would incorporate floral mythologies.[47] He never finished this; but he did finish his book of poetic prose on flowers, *Proserpina*. It is subtitled 'Studies of Wayside Flowers'. It is a book that studies those flowers that fall by the wayside, the flowers that fell from Proserpina's hands when she was abducted by Pluto from her Sicilian garden. It studies what is lost, in order somehow to hold onto it.

Proserpina is the mythical queen, the lost queen. Men write to her through the centuries, offering their flowers, which are her flowers. The poetry is an ever-growing garden of impossible longing.

---

[47] See Elizabeth Campbell, 'Flowers of Evil: Proserpina's Venomous Plants in Ruskin's Botany', *Pacific Coast Philology*, 44 (2009), 114–28 (p. 115).

QUEEN ANNE'S LACE
see 27, 41, 45, 64, 65

I. An herbaceous and biennial plant, the *Daucus carota*'s nomenclature varies from place to place. To some, *wild carrot*. To others, *bird's nest*. Its flowers are small, dull white, and composed of tightly knit rib-like clusters, known as umbels—this word coined in the 1590s from Latin *umbella* meaning 'parasol' or 'sunshade'. Dried umbels detach from the stalk to become what we know as tumbleweeds. The wind blows where it pleases. And the word spoken becomes the breath of life. But do not mistake such familiarity with knowledge: a rapacious weed native to Europe, Queen Anne's lace is easily mistaken for hemlock. For the gift of discernment: breathe in its roots.

II. Note the singular, central dark red flower. This blossom is thought to represent a blood droplet from a needle prick while Queen Anne made lace. Named for both Anne, Queen of Great Britain, and her great grandmother, Anne of Denmark, the white petals of the parasol resemble the lattices of an intricate web, or the buttonhole loop.

III. A plant of contradictions, it is often bedded with the tomato to entice bees, yet it is considered a noxious weed, persisting in the soil for up to five years. Novices often select it for painless planting, also enticed by its rustic beauty and feminine nomenclature. Little do they know a white bed will turn into a white field overnight.

IV.   Her body is not so white as
       anemone petals nor so smooth—nor
       so remote a thing. It is a field
       of the wild carrot taking
       the field by force; [...]

The mimetic quality of William Carlos Williams's poetry is evident in his four flower studies, published in *Sour Grapes* (1921). Here, the poet demonstrates his painting (and planting) techniques by mixing still life and landscape. 'Queen-Anne's Lace' is particularly interesting for its expansive sense of scale, in the same way a Turner lives beyond the frame. The figurative and literal descriptions in this poem are carefully linked, one continual brush stroke, rather than juxtaposed randomly. The poet achieves this effect through a continual use of enjambment; nearly every line of this short, twenty-one-line poem is enjambed; one feels the poem is a continual sentence, or scene. In essence, it is working like a kineograph, or flip book; a moving picture.

The poem begins: 'Her body is not so white as | anemone petals nor so smooth—nor | so remote a thing. It is a field'. By telling us what it is not, we begin to understand what it is, in the same way negative space occupies a black and white photograph. The space around the subject, in this instance the field of 'Queen-Anne's Lace' and not the flower itself, forms a significant shape, which then becomes the real subject of the poem. Perhaps that is why 'a field of the wild carrot' is 'taking the field by force'. Notice Williams's attentive use of the indefinite and definite articles. One reason for 'the' in 'the wild carrot' is that Williams, ever the botanist, is using the article to indicate a specific class among other classes. Queen Anne's lace is classified by some as a noxious weed, and, in this instance, it wildly lives up to its name. But who is overtaking what? The use of 'a' and double use of 'the' draws likely comparisons between both fields. Is this a field of wild carrot taking over another field of wild carrot? Is 'the field' an idealized, quintessential kind of field? I am not sure Williams even knows, which might be why we are left with the last line 'or nothing' as another mode of interpretation. Who (or what) is doing the forcing is unclear because, after all, what is a field but the summation of individual flowers? This grants an unusual sovereignty to the individual flower and its collective. Where does one end and the other begin?

In Japanese, the word *ma* is roughly translated to mean 'gap', 'space', and sometimes 'pause'. It is a spatial concept that is *experienced*, best described as consciousness of place with an awareness of form and non-form. It is the thing that takes place in the imagination and that Williams achieves in this poem through caesura. For example, in these two lines: 'until the whole field is a | white desire, empty, a single stem'. The viewer is stopped mid-sentence to contemplate the beauty of the field. The narrator is struggling to find an appropriate metaphor to describe the field and lands on the abstract: a colour and an emotion. This shift to impressionism suggests the difficulty of putting experiences into words. We see this hesitancy not only with the caesura, but also with the words which follow. Divided by commas, the reader is forced to fall on each grouping as a possibility of interpretation for the metaphor. Ultimately, all (or nothing) becomes the metaphor: 'white desire, empty, a single stem.' In 'Queen-Anne's Lace', it is the silences that give the poem form.

Here, the poet is painter is botanist, giving a precise physical description of the flower: 'white as can be, with a purple mole | at the centre of each flower. | Each flower is a hand's span'. This poem is engaged in seemingly immediate description and self-description, not in apostrophe to the beloved; the flower unfurls under the 'touch' of the sun, as the poem does from the hand that writes it. 'Each part | is a blossom under his touch | to which the fibres of her being | stem one by one': Williams demonstrates the landscape emptying and filling each line of verse. The sexual connotation, too, is unmistakable.

We are taken back to the initial 'force' of the fifth line, and of the poem. It is hard to ignore the masculine presence (and pronoun) throughout it—'Wherever | his hand has lain there is | a tiny purple blemish'—and, for some, the poem can be written off as yet another classical feminization of the female form into a flower, overtaken by the male gaze. To reduce the poem to a feminist interpretation would overlook the very force that drives it (and I do not think it is entirely masculine). The poem rests on the virility and unruly behaviour of Queen Anne's lace. What drives it (and us) is inexplicable. We are forced into and out of this world in the same way. It is difficult to question what came before, or after, because we have always been.

'Here is no question of whiteness' attests to the tautology of the poem. This line grounds the work in a shared reality, something that we can all reasonably agree on (the visual perception of whiteness). Williams is repeating the same conceit using different terminology. It is a kind of circular reasoning, relying on the logic that we can comprehend the epitome of 'whiteness'. Considering Plato's theory of Forms is particularly useful here. In this case, 'whiteness' is a Form because it is unchanging, which makes it objectively perfect according to Plato. Forms transcend time and space, and, through negation, they provide the grounds for beginning, persisting, and ending. A Form is transcendental, and is why Williams emphasizes whiteness six times throughout the poem (usually accompanied by the female possessive determiner, i.e. 'her'). The poet is reflecting nature in attempts to transcend it. What does this suggest about the relationship between 'whiteness' and 'woman'? Here, as Forms, both are inexplicably intertwined, too perfect to fully comprehend. This is also why when Williams has finally exhausted rhetoric, hyperbole, metaphor, he is left with 'nothing'. How does one perfectly describe perfection? Language fails the poet; first the flower is a single stem, then a cluster, then a field. However, it is only the intelligibility of the Form 'whiteness' (and 'woman') that allows us to recognize it, and to attempt to re-render it. Perhaps that is why 'Wherever | his hand has lain there is | a tiny purple blemish'. Perfection is often recognizable in the context of imperfection, negative space. Ultimately, the fact that 'whiteness' is feminised is almost irrelevant; what is more interesting is that 'each part | is a blossom under his touch'. This life-force is symbiotic; it is both masculine and feminine. Even the title, a woman's name, a feminine garment, is at odds, or rather, harmonious, with the flowers' persistent and androgynous temperament.

The first line's negative outline ('Her body is not so white as'), which frames the entirety of the poem. Breaking this line on 'as', along with the rhetorical device, avoids any polarization of the metaphor. Instead, again, a kind of balance is struck. For 'Her body' already contains a metaphoric transformation. If we consider the title as the first line of this poem, the flower then metamorphoses into the female body. An inversion is created: what function can the metaphor serve throughout the poem, if not to call the body back into the form of the flower? These visual elements, as Sharon Dolin suggests in 'Enjambment as Modernist Metaphor in Williams' Poetry', are similar to those that occur in Cubist paintings.[48] In Pablo Picasso's 'Girl with Mandolin' (1910), for example, the foreground and background of the painting merge as the girl and mandolin are transposed. This creates a kind of collage, a two-way visual metaphor, much like Williams's poem. The first line of this poem, particularly the hanging 'as', is foregrounded by the line's edge, and those that follow, like a brush stroke. On first appearance, the painting prescribes no order for reading. 'Queen-Anne's Lace' achieves something very similar through a reverse metaphor: Queen Anne's lace to woman to petals to flower to woman and back to flower. In this case, all roads lead to Rome. As in 'Girl with Mandolin', perspectives switch across the boundaries of lines. A line is infinitely bound until it is broken. Williams explores this thought with his use of *rejets*, accentuated initial words strongly linked to the preceding lines, like 'white' in 'the whole field is a | white desire'. Dolin talks about lines in much the same way that I have discussed negative space. In 'Queen-Anne's Lace' the poetic shape, line length, even the use of the em-dash, all interact in a kind of balance between black and white, positive and negative. We see this structure in evenly weighing phrases like 'the grass | does not raise above it' and 'Each part | is a blossom'. The line is only contained in as much as the field of wild carrot is: as far as our last point of sight. In the space beyond that point there is a new kind of

---

[48] Sharon Dolin, 'Enjambment as Modernist Metaphor in Williams' Poetry', *Sagetrieb* 9 (1990), 31–56.

'field' in which to view the poem and landscape (is it flower as woman or woman as flower?).

The back-and-forth between woman and flower is particularly notable in Williams's use of the word 'stem'. He uses the word twice, once as a verb and once as a noun, with semantic blurring in both instances: to contend with or delay; and, of course, the stalk of a plant. This attests to the poem's metaphorical transpositions and their transformative abilities. The poem continues to ask for transcendence in 'a pious wish to whiteness gone over—', similar to the line 'the grass | does not raise above it'. We are left asking, above what? Over what, to where? And more importantly, what is 'it'? We see here the relational qualities inherent in Plato's theory of Forms, and where mimesis plays a crucial role. Note that Williams is not saying there is a wish to 'white' gone over, but rather 'whiteness', the essence of white. The wish is pious because the poem is a search for something heavenly, a perfect Form. This search entails in desire, a pouring out, then catharsis, only achieved if something is both recognizable yet distant; within reach, yet unobtainable; one flower in a field of flowers. Even if we never find out what 'it' is, the desire to go over it persists.

RHETORIC
see 16, 27, 36, 41, 45, 53, 60, 64, 66, 75

I.   Flowers of Rhethoryke I gathered neauer one,
     As of a pybble to make a preacyous stone.
                                    —William Forrest[49]

II. During the sixteenth century, it was common practice for authors to use the rhetoric of 'gathering'. For instance, the naturalist William Turner's 1548 book is entitled *The names of herbes* [...]. *Gathered by William Turner*.[50] He is credited, or rather credits himself, as a collector not only of botanical specimens but also of words. We see similar titles of the time using the same language; for instance, *The Garden of Health* was 'Gathered by the long experience and industrie of William Langham, practitioner in phisicke'.[51] The verb choice, particularly in Turner's case, is apt, because in order to write the book, he first had to gather the plants themselves.[52] According to Mary Thomas Crane, the cultural significance of 'gathering' as a rhetorical act was well-established in the sixteenth century, for whom gathering was best understood in the process of textual compilation. English Humanism was 'largely based on the collection, assimilation, and redeployment of textual fragments'. A consequence of this palimpsestic approach was a kind of authorship that was collective instead of individual, which, Crane claims, 'fostered a sense of common ownership over texts and ideas'.[53] The rhetoric of 'gathering', then, was embedded in and indebted to a botanical language founded in practice. Three years later, the third volume of Turner's botanical study describes itself as *gathered and made by Wylliam Turner*.[54] The addition of 'made' is notable because it suggests the laborious effort made by its author; after

---

[49] William Forrest, *The history of Grisild the second*, ed. by W. D. Macray (London: Roxburghe Club, 1875), p. 168.

[50] William Turner, *The names of herbes* [...]. *Gathered by William Turner* (London: Steven Mierdman for John Daye and William Seres, 1548).

[51] William Langham, *The garden of health* [...] (London: [The deputies of Christopher Barker], 1597).

[52] See Leah Knight, *Of Books and Botany in Early Modern England: Sixteenth-Century Plants and Print Culture* (Farnham: Ashgate, 2009), pp. 47–49.

[53] Mary Thomas Crane, *Framing Authority: Sayings, Self, and Society in Six-teenth-Century England* (Princeton, NJ: Princeton University Press, 1993), pp. 6–11.

[54] William Turner, *A new herball, wherein are conteyned the names of herbes* [...] *gathered and made by Wylliam Turner* (London: Steven Mierdman, 1551).

all, collecting botanical specimens is not all roses. That a distinction is made between the two is important: 'gathered' and 'made' are not the same thing. Where is the line drawn between the two? The line is blurred despite Turner's discrimination; as botanist, he gathered his plants; as painter, he illustrated their detail; and as writer, he gathered words for the process—and, in that process, remade the plants. His gathering is a kind of remaking.

III. Indeed, he defends his gathering as such. Let us call it the rhetoric of the noble plagiarist, the metaphors of which, fittingly, are themselves borrowed:

> if the honye that the bees gather out of so manye floure of herbes, shrubbes and trees, that are growing in other mennis medowes, feldes and closes: maye iustelye be called the bees honye: and Plinies booke *de naturali historia* maye be called his booke, allthough he haue gathered it oute of so manye good writers whom he vouchsaueth to name in the beginninge of his worke: So maye I call it that I haue learned and gathered of manye good autoures not without great laboure and payne my booke, and namelye because I haue handled no one Autor[.][55]

---

[55] William Turner, preface to *The first and seconde partes of the herbal of William Turner* [...] *set oute with the names of the herbes* [...] (Collen: [the heirs of] Arnold Birckman, 1568), fol. *iiir.

ROSE
see 13, 14, 19, 22, 27, 33, 35, 39, 43, 45, 49, 58, 75

I. 'Now listen! I'm no fool. I know that in daily life we don't go around saying is a is a is a. Yes, I'm no fool; but I think that in that line the rose is red for the first time in English poetry for a hundred years.'[56] So said the self-proclaimed mother of the modern rose, Gertrude Stein. The explanation is as much a rhetorical feat as the line itself: *Rose is a rose is a rose is a rose* (which first appears tucked in the long scroll of 'Sacred Emily', in 1913). No 'red' in any sight but the mind's. Dare one hear instead, in Stein's proclamation, that 'in that line the rose is *read* for the first time in English poetry for a hundred years'?

What, then, do we read? Do we resurrect its meaning in another (though ungrammatical) pun: *a rose is arose*? Is the mere naming of an object a resurrection of it? On one level, the line is a restatement of Aristotle's law of noncontradiction: *(a) rose is a rose* seems to explain as little as *A is A*, until one takes into account the immediate negative implication of the statement: *A is not not-A*. A rose is not not a rose. Stein is attempting to kill the metaphor. The unwelcome blooming of innumerable symbolic and other connotations is what Stein deems cleared away by her declarative rose-circle. A rose is not a woman; a rose is not love; a rose is what it is, which is to say nothing about it, but which is to say it. Nevertheless, one might ask whether, stripped of context and connotation, stripped of connection, it would be possible to understand *rose* at all. If *rose* is the word, and the garden is the world, is the very soil not metaphor?

II. Before the word's semantic obsolescence, Stein suggests, the poet could say *My luve is like a red, red rose* and be in no danger of redundancy. When exactly *rose* is supposed to have become a meaningless word Stein leaves unclear. Still, her apparent ambition to make the rose red again hints at her recognition of the more important word in that line of Burns: *red*.

Before reaching the *red* of the rose, though, it must be acknowledged that the line arose from the soil of *like*. That *like*, that arm of metaphor, stretches for expression. Its exercise is to pull together the heavenly and the earthly, the invisible and the visible, the ineffable and utterance. It creates a relationship in the mind through the senses and the intellect so that an abstract interior understanding, *luve*, can be linked to an external

---

[56] Gertrude Stein, *Four in America* (New Haven, CT: Yale University Press, 1947), p. vi.

object that is seen, smelt, touched. How can love be expressed in words at all? The task is impossible, but even by expressing truly that impossibility, the dimensions of it, the worth of the task becomes more and more evident. A *red, red rose* is somehow infinitely redder than a red rose. Its redness is read twice, in the mind, in the mouth. In other words, no rose is red enough to be like *my luve*, so the only expression is repetition. As in everyday speech. *I love you. I love you.*

III. Eros is eros is eros is eros.

IV.   *Ther is no rose of swych vertù*
       As is the rose that bare Jhesù.

> Ther is no rose of swych vertù
> As is the rose that bar Jhesù;
>   Alleluya.
>   *Ther is etc.*
>
> For in this rose conteynëd was
> Heven and erthe in lytyl space,
>   Res miranda.
>   *Ther is etc.*
>
> Be that rose we may weel see
> That he is God in persones thre,
>   Pari forma.
>   *Ther is etc.*
>
> The aungeles sung the sheperdes to:
> 'Gloria in excelsis Deo.'
>   Gaudeamus.
>   *Ther is etc.*
>
> Leve we all this worldly merthe,
> And folwë we this joyful berthe;
>   Transeamus.
>   *Ther is etc.*[57]

There are many flowers whose names recall the Blessed Virgin Mary:

---

[57] Anonymous, 'Ther is No Rose of Swych Vertù', in *Flora Poetica: The Chatto Book of Botanical Verse*, ed. by Sarah Maguire (London: Chatto & Windus, 2001), p. 260.

lady's keys; *lady's bedstraw*; *marigold*; *lady's-smock*. Mary, according to Pseudo-Jerome, is 'a garden of delights in which are sown all kinds of flowers and spice plants of the virtues'.[58] As Andrea Oliva Florendo notes, in the writings of the early Church, 'the garden imagery of Mary reads like a *florilegium*'.[59] Adam of St Victor's compilation of Marian images in Scripture shows the Biblical roots of this tradition: *a flower without thorns*; *a fountain of the gardens*; *a storehouse of fragrant unguents and pigments*; *a sweet-smelling nard*; *a flower of the field*; *a lily of the valley*; *a celestial paradise*.[60] But the flower perhaps most associated with the Blessed Virgin is the rose.

The hymn above is a carol written around the year 1450. The first two Latin phrases, *res miranda* and *pari forma*, come from the Sequence *Laetabundus*, a hymn sung at Christmastide in the traditional liturgy of the Roman Rite. Most modern annotated editions of 'Ther is no rose' translate the phrase *pari forma* as 'of the same form' or even 'of one substance'; but, significantly, the standard English translation of the *Laetabundus* offers the phrase in its original context as 'in her likeness': that is, God in Mary's likeness. The rose, with its closely knit petals, symbolizes the infolding of the divine and the human. In Mary, God is housed on earth for the first time.

The rose has virtue; though the modern definition of this word also applies, the fifteenth-century audience would have understood *vertù* to mean the remedial power of the plant (as in *OED* sense 8d: 'With reference to a plant, liquid, or other substance: power to affect the body in a beneficial manner; strengthening, sustaining, or healing power'). Its power is spiritual: it raises the mind of the singer to heavenly things, to invocations of *gaudeamus* and *transeamus*: *let us rejoice* and *let us go*. The rose's virtue, its power to do good, lies in something greater than itself. It is no coincidence that, in the refrain, *vertù* rhymes with *Jhesù*.

This rose is a rose that does not stand for itself. It is not self-defining; it is created to an end. It is not stripped of metaphor; it is embellished with it. We cannot comment on what a rose is until we have seen what is hidden within its petals.

---

[58] Pseudo-Jerome, Epistola IX, *De Assumptione Beatæ Mariæ*, cited in Andrea Oliva Florendo, 'The Liturgy of Flowers in a Mary Garden: A Contemplation', in *Mary at the Foot of the Cross, VIII: Coredemptrix, Therefore, Mediatrix of All Graces*, ed. by Peter Damian Fehlner (New Bedford, MA: Academy of the Immaculate, 2008), p. 521.

[59] Andrea Oliva Florendo, 'The Liturgy of Flowers', p. 521.

[60] Attributed to Adam of St Victor; cited in Florendo, 'The Liturgy of Flowers', p. 521.

V. He set before me the book of nature; I understood how all the flowers He has created are beautiful, how the splendor of the rose and the whiteness of the Lily do not take away the perfume of the little violet or the delightful simplicity of the daisy. I understood that if all flowers wanted to be roses, nature would lose her springtime beauty, and the fields would no longer be decked out with little wildflowers.

After my death I will let fall a shower of roses.
—St Thérèse of Lisieux[61]

---

[61] *The Story of a Soul*, trans. by John Clarke (Washington, DC: Institute of Carmelite Studies, 2005), p. 14; *Sœur Thérèse of Lisieux, the Little Flower of Jesus*, trans. by T. N. Taylor (London: Burns, Oates, & Washbourne, 1912), epilogue.

SENTIMENTAL
see 17, 19, 24, 29, 53, 62, 69

I. Jean-Baptiste Monnoyer's *Le Livre de toutes sortes de fleurs d'après nature* depicts flowers with such accuracy that it aided tapestry makers long after his death. Wallace Stevens honours Monnoyer's title in canto IV of 'Esthétique du Mal':

> Livre de Toutes Sortes de Fleurs D'Après Nature.
> All sorts of flowers. That's the sentimentalist.[62]

II. The philosophy behind French formal gardens is not easily translated. William Shenstone shares this sentiment:

> The French use the word "naïve" in such a sense as to be explained by no English word; unless we submit to restrain ourselves in the application of the word "sentimental". It means the language of passion or the heart, in opposition to the language of reflexion and the head.
>
> The most frequent mistake that is made, seems to be that of the means for the end.[63]

This is the end and the beginning of two 'unconnected' thoughts in Shenstone's work; but their proximity, on the page and in their thought, seems to connect them. For Shenstone, gardens are both wild and restrained. Naïvety is sentimental, of the heart; it is as necessary as the head's calm 'reflexion'. Beauty, the 'end' of gardening and of poetry, is eternal; the 'means' must not be confused for it.

> III. Flowers have no sublimity. [...] There is a wide distinction, in general, between flower-loving minds and minds of the highest order. Flowers seem intended for the solace of ordinary humanity: children love them; quiet, tender, contented ordinary people love them as they grow; luxurious and disorderly people rejoice in them gathered: [...] To the child and the girl, the peasant and the manufacturing operative, to

---

[62] Stevens, *Collected Poetry and Prose*, p. 279.
[63] Shenstone, 'Unconnected Thoughts on Gardening', p. 237.

the grisette and the nun, the lover and monk, they are precious always. But to the men of supreme power and thoughtfulness, precious only at times; symbolically and pathetically often to the poets, but rarely for their own sake.

—John Ruskin[64]

---

[64] John Ruskin, *Modern Painters*, 5 vols (London: Smith, Elder and Co., 1873), V, p. 95.

TIME
see 16, 27, 33, 34, 38, 39, 43, 45, 56, 59, 60, 63, 65, 66, 70, 73

I. In Linnaeus's 1751 publication *Philosophia Botanica* he hypothesizes that, if planted correctly, a flower clock could accurately tell time in accordance with flowers that open and close at particular times of the day. He called this garden-plan *Horologium Florae*. Although there are no accounts of Linnaeus planting such a garden, the idea was attempted by many of his nineteenth-century successors with varying degrees of failure. The first mistake: most plants exhibit strong circadian rhythms, meaning few flowers open with predictable regularity. The second mistake involves a simpler oversight; flowering is affected by weather. Lastly, Linnaeus based his assumptions on the flowering times in Uppsala, Sweden, where he taught at university.

II. How well the skilful gardener drew
 Of flow'rs and herbs this dial new;
 Where from above the milder sun
 Does through a fragrant zodiac run;
 And, as it works, th'industrious bee
 Computes its time as well as we.
 How could such sweet and wholesome hours
 Be reckoned but with herbs and flow'rs!
  —Andrew Marvell[65]

---

[65] Andrew Marvell, 'The Garden', in *The Poems of Andrew Marvell*, ed. by Nigel Smith (London: Routledge, 2006), p. 159.

ZINNIA
see 19, 27, 69

I. Named for the German botanist Johann Gottfried Zinn (1727–1759), the zinnia can be found among scrub, or in dry grassland. The flower, a member of the daisy family, comes in a delightful array of shapes, from linear to ovate, dome-shaped, oblong, and convex. It also boasts a wide range of colours: purple, lilac, red, orange, chartreuse, and white.

II. Zinnias are planted in spring and flower in summer. They make excellent companion plants for their uncanny ability to attract butterflies and hummingbirds. A natural defence against whiteflies, the zinnia's long stalk can reach heights of one hundred centimetres. Most species have sturdy, erect stems but some have a careless habit of spreading perpendicularly over the ground.

III. Louis Zukofsky published *80 Flowers* in 1976, a testament to his wife's garden:

> With prayer-plant eyes annually winter-leggy
> zinnia miracles itself perennial return [...] [66]

The highly condensed poem begins 'With'. We accompany the poet into the natural world with reverence. The monosyllabics of 'prayer-plant eyes' become a funeral procession of words because we are heralding the death of the plant. The zinnia is on its last leg, or, as our poet puts it, 'winter-leggy'. Although the subject of this first line could be a number of things (is the reader 'winter-leggy' or is it the zinnia's stems?), the subject of the poem is certain. The transition of time for our poet is a fact, yet it is a difficult one to fix or place, especially during the long winter months.

But then, as Zukofsky describes, something extraordinary happens. The zinnia 'miracles itself'. It is a rare occurrence to will oneself into existence; but the zinnia is a self-seeding plant. Zukofsky seems to know this about the botanical properties of the zinnia. He also knows it is a perennial, suggesting the doubled-over miraculousness of the zinnia because it not only spreads its own seed but raises itself out of the ground every year. A must for lazy gardeners.

---

[66] Louis Zukofsky, 'Zinnia', cited in Mark Scroggins, *The Poem of a Life: A Biography of Louis Zukofsky* (New York, NY: Shoemaker Hoard, 2007), p. 457.

The timing of the lines is just as important as the timing of each blossoming. 'Blest interim strength lengthening' mimics this process. The line repeats itself in cadence, with a single stressed syllable followed by a dactyl. A natural pause is forced between 'blest interim' and 'strength lengthening' as the words do what they say; a transition from winter to summer, a pause between 'interim' and 'strength'. Like the stalk of the zinnia, time and nature stretch into 'coreopsis'-summers', a triumph of life over death.

Zukofsky seems to combine Imagist and Symbolist techniques as the poem's 'rampant riming between the lines and the world 'outside' the lines' is expressed with compounded urgency. The line 'actual some time whereso near' expresses as much, distilling each word to its sonic and symbolic meaning, creating a new image of the 'outside' world through sounds where only existing images may have failed. The inability to fix time pervades here, too. Varying kinds of expression are used in reference to time (the word itself falling directly in the middle of the sentence), from 'actual' to 'near', suggesting that all and none of these words are describing a moment. Time is difficult to place during winter because of the absence of life; it is one form of eternity into another. Yet here, in spring, time is difficult to pin down because of the excess of life. A rapid succession of words reflects the dramatically changing landscape throughout the poem. Each word seems to burst from the ground.

By the end of the poem, a cycle has been completed as we revisit 'white night'. This return is habitual, like the 'currents tide', like night into day. 'Zinnia' is the final poem of Zukofsky's garden-sequence, a word that begins with 'z' and ends with 'a'.

ACKNOWLEDGEMENTS

'Dies Natalis' was published by *The Dark Horse*, in Volume 40, Winter & Spring 2019.

'My Mother the Dishwasher' and 'Lot's Wife' were published in the *Coast to Coast to Coast* pamphlet competition, 2018.

'Penny Wedding' appeared in the *You Don't Look British* anthology, 2018.

'Some Definitions' appeared in *Split 580*, 2016.

'Antonyms' and 'Lorem Ipsum' appeared in *Zyzzyva*, 2015.

'Interruption and Completion of a Thought,' Glasgow Haiku,' The Child Dreaming in a Poet's House,' On Heidegger's *Being and Time*,' 'Flora and Fauna,' 'Colloquy with a Closed Window,' 'Glesga Prayer,' 'Lessons on How to Understand a Famous Painting,' 'Lot's Wife,' 'Danaë,' 'Isle of Skye,' and 'The Loves of Plants' appeared in *New Poetries VI*, Carcanet, 2015.

'Lessons on How to Understand a Famous Painting' appeared in *Aesthetica* Creative Writing Annual, 2014.

'Elegy for Emma,' 'The Gallery,' 'Sunday,' 'Listening to Scriabin for the First Time,' and 'Oceanic' appeared in *Agenda*, Broadsheet No. 23, 2014.

'The Child Dreaming in a Poet's House' appeared in *Fish Poetry Prize Anthology*, 2014.

'Glesga Prayer' appeared in *PN Review* 214, Volume 40 Number 2, November-December, 2013.

'Danaë', 'Interruption and Completion of a Thought', and 'Lessons on How to Understand a Famous Painting' appeared in *PN Review* 209, Volume 39 Number 3, January-February, 2013.

www.ingramcontent.com/pod-product-compliance
Lightning Source LLC
Chambersburg PA
CBHW030905170426
43193CB00009BA/740